Workplace Jazz

Workplace Jazz

How to IMPROVISE–9 Steps to Creating High-Performing Agile Project Teams

Gerald J. Leonard

Leader in applied, concise business books

Workplace Jazz: How to IMPROVISE–9 Steps to Creating
High-Performing Agile Project Teams

Cover Image licensed by Chad Barr, President of The Chad Barr Group.
https://www.thechadbarrgroup.com
https://www.chadbarrphotography.com

Interior design by Exeter Premedia Services Private Ltd., Chennai, India

First published in 2021 by
Business Expert Press, LLC
222 East 46th Street, New York, NY 10017
www.businessexpertpress.com

ISBN-13: 978-1-95334-948-4 (paperback)
ISBN-13: 978-1-95334-949-1 (e-book)

Business Expert Press Portfolio and Project Management Collection

Collection ISSN: 2156-8189 (print)
Collection ISSN: 2156-8200 (electronic)

First edition: 2021

10 9 8 7 6 5 4 3 2 1

Printed in the United States of America.

Description

In *Workplace Jazz*, I hope to raise a battle cry for individual and corporate responsibility in building cultures that are both healthier and more productive for those working in them.

Workplace Jazz teaches the strategies and steps professionals need to connect and transform their agile project teams and execute for optimum results. According to McKinsey, "Research shows that hurtful workplace behavior can depress performance, increase employee turnover, and even mar customer relationships. And that Workplace relationships may be fraying as fewer employees work in the office and feel more isolated and less respected."

The gap between workforce engagement and workplace productivity is widening. In a study conducted by Kronos and Future Workplace, "The biggest threat to building an engaged and transformational workforce in 2017 is employee burnout. The newest study in the Employee Engagement Series conducted by Kronos Incorporated and Future Workplace® found 95 percent of human resource leaders admit employee burnout is sabotaging workforce retention, yet there is no obvious solution on the horizon." When teams are emotionally connected and supportive, burnout is reduced, and engagement goes up.

What should leaders do to address this workforce engagement and productivity gap? Should companies keep implementing culture improvement processes and procedures that do not address the emotional connection that teams need? Should they just accept the status quo and try to keep moving forward?

Workplace Jazz offers a step-by-step process enhanced with stories, research, mini case studies, metaphors, and a strategic blueprint for developing connected and transformational project teams based on the author's experiences as a professional musician and certified business consultant. The author will also include stories from a highly skilled set of guest contributors who are both musicians and some well-known business authors and consultants.

Agile transformational project teams are critical to your workplace because they enable your staff to work well under pressure, they are less defensive, they are more open to feedback, and they want to understand each other and are more supportive. *Workplace Jazz offers insights into how to help your teams become successful agile transformational project teams using the IMPROVISE framework to grow in the areas of emotional and conversational intelligence while experiencing the connections that professional musicians achieve when they are performing.*

Keywords

workplace; productivity; project management; agile project management; agile project teams; team transformation; organizational culture; agile transformation; continuous learning; lifelong learning; performance reviews; workplace engagement; effective communication; risk management; continuous growth; agile leadership; effective leadership

Contents

Endorsements

"Congratulations, Gerald, on your new book. You have obviously put a lot of heart into it. This wonderful, enjoyable book entertains you and opens your mind and heart to inspiring others. It can change your life and the lives of others." —**Brian Tracy, Author/Speaker/Consultant**

"Gerald! I'm so proud of you! What a great creative approach for your book!" —**Jolley By Design!, Dee Taylor-Jolley | COO, CFO**

"I love music and I love business. When you put them together in a book, as Gerald Leonard has done, you have an interesting, entertaining, and informative combination that makes for a great book. Leonard has the chops as a musician and is savvy in business. The lessons in this book will teach you to build and manage a team that is engaged and productive. That's music to any leader's ears." —**Shep Hyken, customer service/experience expert and New York Times bestselling author of The Amazement Revolution**

"In his latest book, Workplace Jazz, Gerald J. Leonard provides fresh new insights and practical tools that will allow leaders to adapt their organizations and to develop agile transformation project teams to excel in the new world of constant change." —**Antonio Nieto-Rodriguez, Author, Speaker, Thinkers50, past PMI Chair**

"Who would have thought of tying jazz and the workplace together? Well, Gerald Leonard has, and he does a great job of integrating how a business can use the jazz concepts to flourish in these crazy times. He's great at conducting us in reaching new levels of success." —**Jerry V. Teplitz, JD, PhD, Author of Switched-On Selling: Balance Your Brain for Sales Success and Managing Your Stress in Difficult Times: Succeeding in Times of Change**

"Wow. Your passion for music and agile project management oozes from the pages. I found it inspiring. I love your conversational writing style. It makes for a very comfortable read. I also think your general chapter approach of stories, theory, and application works really well." —**Rob Tieman, P.E., Director, Project Management Office (PMO), Virginia Department of Transportation**

"Gerald has done a magnificent job in highlighting the connection between building a great jazz ensemble and building high-performing projects and business teams. Teams capable of developing and encouraging a healthier and more productive workplace culture. I'm pleased to have Gerald as a regular writer on our team of project management experts at PMWorld 360 Magazine, writing about what he knows best—workplace culture!" —**Moira Alexander, PMP, I.S.P., ITCP/IP3P, Founder and Editor-in-Chief of PMWorld 360 Magazine, Founder of Lead-Her-Ship Group, and author of LEAD or LAG: Linking Strategic Project Management & Thought Leadership**

"Workplace Jazz has a universal theme and will appeal to those in music and in business. As drummer, who's performed with Gerald, I feel this comparison between jazz musicians and agile teams makes for a great read. The insights in the book will teach you how to create a high-performing team. Bravo Gerald!" —**Bill Cates, CSP, CPAE, Author of Radical Relevance**

"Creating a high-performing team is key to any business, game, or sport. Workplace Jazz shows you how to do it by demonstrating world-class musicians using their talents and skills to build great teams. Gerald makes it plain and clear how we can adopt the concepts, principles, and practices of these great jazz musicians to build world-class high-performing teams in our organizations. I'm immensely glad that Gerald has published his unique and fresh insights towards the much-studied field of building high-performing agile teams." —**Yu-kai Chou, International Keynote Speaker on Gamification and Behavioral Design, Creator of the Octalysis Framework**

Foreword

Workplace Culture and the Business Plan

Every organization has both a workplace culture and a plan. The workplace culture exists whether it has been crafted intentionally or just allowed to grow organically. Intentional cultures, as we have seen at Disney, Apple, Zappos, the U.S. Marines, and major religious institutions, are built around a shared set of beliefs, a universal set of standards, and a vision of the optimum outcome or dreamed-of status. An organic culture would not create a harmonious result. Instead, it would produce chaos.

Your Culture Is the Bass in Your Organization

Likewise, every organization has a plan. The trouble is, some of those plans are no plans at all; they are merely accepting the random flow of circumstances and hoping for the best, rather than creating the conditions necessary for success. The familiar adage is: If you fail to plan, you are planning to fail. By the way, hope is not a plan. Hope is wishing. It is like those who say my self-motivation strategy is procrastination. I create the urgency to get myself to act. Procrastination is not a strategy; it is a slave-master. Only an intentional and well-thought-out plan is incredibly useful in an organization.

The Plan Is the Drums in Your Band

Gerald Leonard is a professional musician. Correction, he is a professional *and* he is a musician. He brings the qualities of both disciplines to everything he does. When he is managing systems in an organization, he is informed by his musical training and artistry. When he is performing in a symphony or jazz ensemble, he is guided by his knowledge of systems theory and organizational behavior. For that reason, I believe he is the perfect person to write this book. I have learned from him, and I have had the privilege of sharing the stage with him musically. Gerald is the rock that allows the rest of us to ... well, Rock!

I recommend this book for you and your team. Read it together and discuss each part of it. Become the Ensemble of Achievement that you are collectively capable of becoming.

In the Spirit of Harmony,

Jim Cathcart, CSP, CPAE

Sales and Marketing Hall of Fame, author of 18 books, including the international bestsellers *The Acorn Principle*, *Relationship Selling*, and the new *The Self-Motivation Handbook*.

Founder and CEO of www.Cathcart.com

Preface

The title of this book is *Workplace Jazz*.

In these pages, I hope to raise a battle cry for individual and corporate responsibility in building cultures that are both healthier and more productive for those working in them.

First, a definition: a healthier and more productive culture is a culture that attracts, inspires, and retains great people. It also builds brand ambassadors among team members and customers. People who work for the company or buy from it admire the company and love to talk about it and its products.

I have chosen the words "Workplace Jazz" very carefully and for a reason: most companies now are having to compete in an environment where technology skills, computer skills, project management skills, and technology leadership skills are paramount. Managing high performers on high-technology teams is exactly like conducting a jazz ensemble. As we will demonstrate in this book, there is a direct comparison.

But, an overwhelming amount of evidence also shows that employee engagement or happiness across all industries and jobs is at an all-time low. The needle does not seem to be moving at all, no matter how much anyone talks about the need for greater *employee engagement*.

Even the CEO of Gallup, Jim Clifton, reposted an article on LinkedIn that essentially said: "Your workforce is not engaged. So please find an employee engagement tool and use it. Find out what is wrong and do something about it."

The message was not "use a Gallup tool." It was, instead, please just find a tool, any tool, and do something. Anything.

Why should we be alarmed about low rates of engagement?

We should be alarmed because leadership training simply has not kept up with the dynamics of the changing workforce.

In brief, the hallmark traits of high performers in software development, or most IT professions, are almost identical to those of an artist: creativity is the most essential trait, followed by the need to work on

a great team, in a respectful environment that recognizes cultural differences, among intelligent colleagues who have learned to collaborate
effectively—even if, and especially if, that means arguing and disagreeing.
Just as long as you make the conflict *creative and collaborative.*

In the mind of an artist, especially one who is employed in a jazz
ensemble, there are only two kinds of performances—great performances
and horrible performances. There is no gray area for high performers. It's
either great or it is shameful.

The problem is, too many leaders in today's companies don't have
a clue as to the artistic temperaments of their team members, and even
fewer have a clue as to how to manage them.

It is this problem that we intend to tackle head-on in this book.

Before proceeding, we will make one more critical point:

Most of the lack of engagement in the workforce today can be traced
to two problems: a lack of understanding and a lack of communication.
Most people, when asked, say that they do not believe anyone who man-
ages them has the slightest clue what they are interested in, what they
are passionate about, what they could be doing to make the company
better, and what training and feedback they need to make them better.
Performance management reviews are notoriously cryptic and un-useful,
and many of them should be banned just from the sheer lack of construct
validation. In plain terms, they aren't worth the paper they are printed on,
or the computer byte space they take up.

This Book Is About YOU

When I say this book is about you, I mean it as both a fact and a challenge.

What I mean is this: Since so much of our leadership has not caught
on to what is required of a truly engaged workforce, I believe it is time for
all team members to step up to the plate and to voice their concerns about
the lack of communication in the workplace today.

Before you do that, though, you need to take careful stock of what
concerns you and of what might make you happier in your working environment if things were to change.

Many people I talk to have grown so numb from lack of meaningful
conversations at work that they almost seem to have forgotten what it is

that caused them to get an education, learn skills, and enter the working world in the first place.

So, a few apparent questions I will ask in the course of this introduction and this book are as follows:

- What is it you are most passionate about?
- What are your most vital skills?
- In the "jazz ensemble" of your team, where might your skills shine the brightest, if they were truly appreciated, recognized, and trained?
- Do you feel you have strong leadership or a great conductor?
- If not, where does the leadership need to be improved?

These are issues that *must* be brought to leadership today. Someone has to have the courage to stand up and say:

"We do not know what our people are good at and what they are concerned about. We do not know how they can be made to feel more engaged. We hardly know anything about them at all. Our teams are not 'agile,' and we do not honestly know how to bring out the best in our team as a whole, or to foster and lead true collaboration and creative conflict. And that must change."

We have to say this because it is *the* problem and the problem is not being fixed. If it is good enough for the Gallup CEO, Jim Clifton, to point out as a hint, then perhaps we can all accept it as our most critical mission as well.

So Where Is the Bass—and Why Can't I Hear the Drums?

If you ever spend time in a recording studio, you will notice two things being said all the time, and far more frequently than any other thing:

1. The bass doesn't sound right. It needs to be more solid. It isn't EQed properly. It sounds muddy. We need to work on that.
2. Turn up the drums! I can't hear them! And what's with that lousy kick drum sound? We need to work on those drums and turn them up!

As Meghan Trainor said in her popular and very true song, "It's All About That Bass." Though I might add: and the drums.

Musical engineers spend more time on the bass and the drums than they do anything else. There is a reason for that. It is the bass sound and the drum sound that are most responsible for making a song danceable, making it a hit, and making people keep the song on when it comes on the radio, instead of turning it off or changing channels.

In a recording studio, you will hear loud noises: loud laughter, loud shouting, loud arguing, loud bass, and loud drums. People will fight—in a friendly way—over the sound of that bass and those drums. But they are supposed to fight. If you put out a song that has a lousy bass part and a lousy drum sound, you are dead. No one is going to buy it. Your song will tank. You have wasted all of your money, and the public is not going to dance to your song. You will not make the billboard charts.

The culture of the organization you create is just like the bass, and the business plan is like the drums.

I titled my first book *Culture Is the Bass* for this reason: The culture of the organization you create is just like the bass, and the business plan is like the drums. People need to be able to hear the beat. They need to be able to follow the beat. The rhythm should make them get up and dance, not sit there and drool.

Furthermore, musicians are not afraid to confront the "deadly sins" of recording. They want to face them head-on and with brutal honesty before they record a song and release it. They don't want butterflies and kittens from their producer. They want the truth!

And here are some of the questions they might ask:

What's the hook of this song?
What makes it catchy?
Why will people relate?
How did these musicians get into this room?

Why can't I hear the drums?

Why does the song seem to ignore everything popular on the radio?

Does anyone here know what people are listening to these days?

And so on.

If you are in business and running a business team in software, IT, or almost any other field and you are not asking the same questions (or very similar ones), you are in big trouble.

This book will methodically teach you how to apply all of the lessons we can learn from building a great jazz ensemble to building a great company and great teams within that company.

Why You Need a Workplace Jazz Culture

Workplace Jazz teaches the strategies and steps professionals need to connect and transform their agile project teams and execute for optimum results. According to McKinsey, "Research shows that hurtful workplace behavior can depress performance, increase employee turnover, and even mar customer relationships. And that Workplace relationships may be fraying as fewer employees work in the office and feel more isolated and less respected."

The gap between workforce engagement and workplace productivity is widening. In a study conducted by Kronos and Future Workplace, "The biggest threat to building an engaged and transformational workforce in 2017 is employee burnout. The newest study in the Employee Engagement Series conducted by Kronos Incorporated and Future Workplace® found 95 percent of human resource leaders admit employee burnout is sabotaging workforce retention. Yet, there is no obvious solution on the horizon." When teams are emotionally connected and supportive, burnout is reduced, and engagement goes up.

What should leaders do to address this workforce engagement and productivity gap? Should companies keep implementing culture improvement processes and procedures that do not address the emotional connection that teams need? Should they just accept the status quo and try to keep moving forward?

Workplace Jazz offers a step-by-step process enhanced with stories, research, mini case studies, metaphors, and a strategic blueprint for developing connected and high-performing project teams based on my experience as a professional musician and certified business consultant. I will also include stories about world-class artist, jazz musicians, and from a highly skilled set of guest contributors who are musicians, well-known business authors and consultants.

High-Performing Agile Project Teams are critical to your workplace because they enable your staff to work well under pressure, they are less defensive, they are more open to feedback, and they want to understand each other and are more supportive. Workplace Jazz offers insights into how to help your teams become successful High-Performing Agile Project Teams using the IMPROVISE framework to grow in the areas of emotional and conversational intelligence while experiencing the connections that professional musicians achieve when they're performing in their peak performance zone.

Acknowledgments

I am extremely grateful for the team at Bradley Communication: Steve and Bill Harrison, Debra Englander, Martha Bullen, and Geoffrey Berwind for their wisdom, insight, and coaching. I am thankful for my literary agent, John Willig, and my publishing editor, Timothy J. Kloppenborg, PhD, PMP, PMI-ACP at Business Expert Press.

This book is dedicated to my son Kenon and daughter Peyton for loving me through my personal growth and journey.

Also, to my Mom and Dad, Lola J. Leonard and the late Willie C. Leonard, for without their love, compassion, and discipline, I would not be the man I have become. Thanks, Mom, for taking me to music lessons as soon as you came home from work.

Additionally, to my siblings, Deborah D. Leonard, Sharon L. Stevens, Wendell L. Leonard, the late Harold L. Leonard, and Carolyn Leonard, for protecting me, guiding me, and putting up with me. I love you deeply.

Finally, to my wife Edith Leonard, for loving me through my journey of bringing this book to life and loving me for who I am.

CHAPTER 1

What Can Music Teach Us?

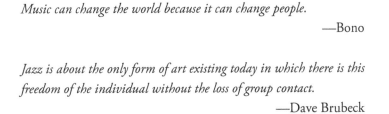

Music can change the world because it can change people.

—Bono

Jazz is about the only form of art existing today in which there is this freedom of the individual without the loss of group contact.

—Dave Brubeck

This chapter will teach you the concept, principles, and framework for creating a workplace jazz environment.

Now, before I get into the concepts, principles, and frameworks, let me share with you how I discovered the power of music and what it has taught me throughout my life and is still teaching me today.

During my childhood, the world experienced the Cuban Missile Crisis, the assassinations of President John F. Kennedy and civil rights icon Martin Luther King Jr., and the Vietnam War. It was a challenging time in our history and the world that I grew up in.

I would often sneak away from all the noise, sit in the closet in my home, and grab my sister's red guitar with the white tuning knobs. She did not know I wanted to play it, so I had to sneak in her room and sit in the closet and play.

Finally, one day, she found me, and she realized she was never going to play that little red guitar, so she let me have it ... in more ways than one. Since that time, I have not had to sneak her guitar, and I fell in love with learning to play. Music has taught me many things: the discipline of practice, playing fairly with friends, how to listen, how to connect with others, and how to have fun.

I joined a band with some friends, and one of them was a fantastic guitar player, and I then realized that to stay in the group, I had to learn to play the bass guitar and up my game; I had to learn to practice in a whole new way. When playing the guitar, I simply played chords and rhythms, and practice was more casual. Taking up the bass forced me to realize the structure of the song and the foundation, and it dawned on me that I had to find a new approach to practicing the bass. And, this experience has laid the foundation for what music has taught me my entire life.

I have spent a large part of my life studying music since learning to play the bass. I have also spent time overcoming some of the myths about music. Myths like:

- Certain music genres, like classical music, require that you can only learn them by receiving formal training.
- Classically trained musicians are intellectually more superior then non-classically trained musicians.
- Listening to classical music as a child will make you smarter and improve your intelligence quotient (IQ).

What I have come to learn is that music has a compounding effect, like investing money and receiving interest. When you spend time studying music, practicing, rehearsing with others, and performing, music will have a powerful effect on reshaping your brain and enhancing your ability to think.

Researchers at the University of Vermont College of Medicine analyzed the brain scans of 232 healthy children ages 6 to 18 years. They were specifically looking at brain development in kids who play instruments.

"What we found was the more a child trained on an instrument," said James Hudziak, a professor of psychiatry at the University of Vermont and director of the Vermont Center for Children, Youth, and Families, "it accelerated cortical organization in attention skill, anxiety management, and emotional control."

Music gives a soul to the universe, wings to the mind, flight to the imagination and life to everything.
—Plato High-Performance Secrets from the Philadelphia Jazz
Curators—Donald Robinson and Gerald Veasley

Music is like a sage advisor. It is a gift that we have been given. It can shape who we are and how we relate to each other, and it will enhance our abilities and develop our minds. More than anything, music connects us. Music brings us together. It helps us to relate to one another in a way that nothing else can. Music has the power to heal.

I once had an opportunity, after going to a networking meeting in the Philadelphia area, to visit some friends that I had met a few years earlier. The leader of the networking event introduced me to the piano player at his church. I thought he was just a standard musician, classical or gospel pianist. When I finally met the gentleman, his name was Donald Robinson. Well, Donald happened to be a Grammy-nominated producer, and he works very closely with named Gerald Veasley. Gerald Veasley is a world-class bassist.

After meeting them, I got to know Donald and built a friendship with him, and they have created an environment within the Philadelphia area that is amazing. They create wonderful music, they are curators, and they have many of the top smooth jazz headliners coming and working with them regularly.

Gerald Veasley was a bassist for Grover Washington Jr. for many years. He has also played with McCoy Tyner, the Jaco Pastorius Big Band, Gerald Levert, Teddy Pendergrass, and many, many others. Gerald, with his wife Roxanne and daughter, established a regular event at the SOUTH Restaurant in Philadelphia called Unscripted Jazz Series at SOUTH Jazz Parlor. And Donald, as a Grammy-nominated producer, has worked with the likes of Kurt Weyland, Kim Waters, Najee, Stevie Wonder, Will Downing, Walter Beasley, Eric Darius, and many others. He has produced number one hits on the billboard charts for the likes of Rachelle Ferrell, Vanessa Williams, Phyllis Hyman, Nancy Wilson, Gladys Knight, and many more.

These two music curators have taken their love for music and are collaborating with other world-class musicians, and they are giving back. They set up their business in a way that they reach out to up-and-coming artists, and they give back. You see, music has taught them that it is not just about having all the accolades of being Grammy-nominated and playing with all the headliners; it is about becoming more than you were yesterday. It is about giving back, giving back to your community and society. They have laid the groundwork for many young, new musicians to learn jazz and to grow.

Gerald has even created a yearly Bass Bootcamp where Grammy-nom-inated bassists like Marcus Miller, Victor Wooten, and many others have come and shared their knowledge with other bassists, whether they are a working professional or a beginner. You see, music can bring us together, and it does not require a lot of us to make a difference with music. It can be done with just a few, and that is the point I want to make about what music can teach us. We can develop critical skills, concepts, and mind-sets by using our talents and sharing the knowledge we have been given through music. If we are not musicians, we can take the principles of what music teaches and embed it in our hearts, and it will help us to grow, to change, to think, and to give back.

To learn more about Donald Robinson and Gerald Veasley, you can check out their websites at https://sowmusiconline.org/home and https://geraldveasley.com/, respectively.

According to dictionary.com, Music is defined as "an art of sound in time that expresses ideas and emotions in significant forms through the elements of rhythm, melody, harmony, and color. Music is the tones or sounds employed, occurring in single line (melody) or multiple lines (harmony), and sounded or to be sounded by one or more voices or instruments, or both."

The word *music* has its origins from the Greek word *mousikè*, which means téchnē (the art) of the muse.

To muse, according to the original Greek language, means to "think or meditate in silence, as on some subject, or to comment thoughtfully or ruminate upon."

So, now that you know what the term *music* means, can you see the power of music when you hear your favorite song, and you experience thoughts, memories, and a physical and emotional change? Music takes on a life of its own and moves you to feel happy or sad, reflection, or energized.

Jazz music is America's past and its potential, summed up and sancti-fied and accessible to anybody who learns to listen to, feel, and under-stand it. The music can connect us to our earlier selves and our better selves-to-come. It can remind us of where we fit on the timeline of human achievement, an ultimate value of art.

—Wynton Marsalis, an American virtuoso trumpeter, composer,
teacher, and artistic director of jazz at Lincoln Center

The Neuroscience of Music

I've never known a musician who regretted being one. Whatever deceptions life may have in store for you, the music itself is not going to let you down.

—Virgil Thomson, composer

According to the National Institute of Health (NIH), "Music performance requires facility in sensory and cognitive domains, combining skills in auditory perception, kinesthetic control, visual perception, pattern recognition, and memory."

NIH researchers have concluded that short- or long-term musical training has a positive impact on one's "neural, cognitive, and communication function."

Also, according to NIH, "Adult instrumental musicians, for example, have more gray matter in somatosensory, premotor, superior parietal, and inferior temporal areas of the cortex and these enlargements correlate with their levels of expertise (Gaser and Schlaug 2003). Musicians also have larger cerebellar volume, with the extent of this greater volume correlating with the lifelong intensity of musical practice, which has been proposed to be due to the role of the cerebellum in motor and cognitive skill learning (Hutchinson et al. 2003)."

In another NIH study, "Six-month-old infants were randomly assigned either to an active music class consisting of group activities and playing simple instruments or to a passive music class where they listened to music but played no instruments. After six months of training, the infants in the active group demonstrated enhanced enculturation to Western tonal pitch structure, enhanced brain responses to musical tones, and increased social development relative to the listening group (Gerry et al. 2012; Trainor et al. 2012)."

Music can change our brains.

Skill practice in music or any other discipline has the power to transform our brains through the neural plasticity.

Infants who experience musical training together develop in a way that increases their social skills. Because our brains have the capacity for neural plasticity or to be moldable, adult project teams can use musical exercises to improve neurological and social skills.

Here are ten things music can teach us about life if we are willing to listen:

1. Our relationships with each other define us, and we accomplish more by working together. Music creates a social environment that allows us to engage and collaborate while transcending our cultural biases.

2. We have other forms of communication other than words. Music allows us to communicate in nonverbal ways that can reach into our very souls.

3. Life is finite. Life, like music, has a beginning and an end. To truly enjoy life, we must appreciate the journey, smell the roses, and reflect on our experiences. Listening to music allows us to enjoy the ride of where the music wants to take us. We get to relish in its sounds, tones, and melodies and reflect on how it makes us feel.

4. The only consistency in life is change. Your previous life experiences shape the way you view current and future events. Music that you have listened to in the past will sound different and have a different meaning in the future because you have changed and gained new perspectives.

5. Objects in life can be symbolic and represent other things. With music, we get to decide for ourselves what the music means. Each person can have their interpretation of what the music means to them. It is up to us to give it a meaning for ourselves.

6. In the same way that a piece of music can be interpreted by a different artist and performed in different ways, the same idea can be understood and produce different outcomes.

7. Music has the power to make us happy, sad, mad, or glad by the tone, pitch, and melody of the song. Other people can, in the same way, affect our emotions and outlook.

8. Hearing theme music from one of our favorite TV shows alerts us to what is coming on next. Because we are familiar with the melody, we are confident that we understand what is happening. Listening to music that we are familiar with is like developing habits; the more we repeatedly do something, the more comfortable we become with it.

9. Music also alerts us to the power of change. When we hear an unusual tone or rhythm, we become aware of a change in the song.

In life, when we experience something different or unique, we recognize it as a potential change, and the new experience reminds us that change is the only constant in life.

10. Finally, music teaches us the power of perspective. When we hear different instruments playing and interacting around the same melodic phrase or tune, we are listening to different perspectives of a song. The instruments have a conversational approach, and we are reminded of the process of sharing, discussing, and being in a dialog with others. It is through the process of exchanging ideas and conversations that we explore, learn, and grow. Music reminds us of our need to be open to different perspectives because it expands our mental horizons.

Music Can Teach Us How to Think Agile

Imagine going to a music performance, there are four world-class musicians on stage, and they are your favorites. Maybe it is Najee. Maybe it is Kurt Weyland or Boney James or Gerald Albright, and he has his band, and the band kicks off, and they start playing, and they play the melody, which is simple but straightforward and fast and aggressive. And then, Gerald steps up to the mic. The band gets quiet, and he starts to interpret and create his melodies around the rhythms and exchanges of the song. All the other musicians are listening intently and following along. You see, music can teach us how to think agile. What is agile? Agile is a mindset. Being agile is a way of being nimble and flexible in how we think. There are processes and methodologies and frameworks around being agile; it is more than just doing agile. To be agile, we must become agile. We must learn to think agile.

Agile is a mindset. Being agile is a way of being nimble and flexible in how we think.

In the same way, more than just making music, when you make music, it sounds mechanical and structured. But, when you think musically, you can play "Mary Had a Little Lamb" and play it mechanically, and it sounds like the nursery rhyme, "Mary Had a Little Lamb." Or you can think musically and play "Mary Had a Little Lamb" in such a way that your audience turns around and weeps. Music can help us to think agile.

In my experience, I have discovered six benefits that agile thinking provides:

1. Agile thinking increases an organization's return on investment.
2. It delivers a reliable result and helps us to be able to handle uncertainty.
3. It unleashes creativity and innovation.
4. It allows the groups to hold each other accountable.
5. It boosts performance.
6. It improves the group's effectiveness and reliability.

There are many frameworks and many processes around agile, and we will get into them. There are things like epics, features, user stories, and acceptance criteria. There are scrum processes, and there is the upside-down triangle where cost and time are fixed, and scope is variable. And, these are important, but this gets into some of the processes of doing agile. But, what this book is about is using the metaphor of music to help you build the framework in your mind and your team's mind so that you begin to think and become agile; that you, in your essence, become agile. And, when everyone on your team becomes agile in their thinking in a natural way, then the organization becomes agile, and we begin to do business in an agile manner.

What is jazz, and how does the agile mindset apply? As I shared earlier, jazz is the combination of musicians working together to express, listen, support, and hold each other accountable and share their interpretation of a particular musical selection. That is why, you can have one band play "Tonight in Tunisia," and it sounds one way, and you can have another band play "Tonight in Tunisia," and it sounds a different way.

What is workplace jazz? Workplace jazz is developing the jazz mindset, an agile mindset, and bringing it into your work culture and creating teams of like-minded agilest where everyone becomes an expert in their craft. At the same time, they understand the bigger vision and the value that they create. They buy into the process, and they are open to supporting, listening, working together, and creating beautiful music, in a way that they could not do by themselves.

What follows is a summation of how the rest of the book will flow and a description of the IMPROVISE framework:

1. **Improving Your Skills: Deliberate Practice**: Creating a high-performing team culture is based on developing trust, building conversational skills, and understanding the neuroscience of conversations, which requires improving your communication and listening skills like a jazz musician.

2. **Measure What Matters**: Use an incremental approach to implementing agile. People can accept small changes over time. Focus each increment on the core objectives and key results (OKRs).

3. **Cultivating Positive Attitudes**: Change happens, then the team has to focus on transitioning to the change to make it the new normal. Musicians are impacted by the mirror neuron effect when they work together. When you see another musician overcome a musical challenge, you are more likely to feel confident that you can overcome it as well. Jazz musicians also tend to imitate each other during the performance; this is based on the mirror neuron effect.

4. **From Risk to Reward**: Take the retrospective review session to a deeper level to ingrain the learning for the team. Every performance is an opportunity to learn for a jazz musician. They are consistently discussing what is working and what is not working.

5. **Open to Feedback**: Jazz is a language that jazz musicians are consistently learning to speak better through their instruments. Jazz musicians are also consistently learning from each other as they perform and practice.

6. **Visualize Your Results**: Engage experts who have real-world experience. They will act as tour guides and not travel agents. Jazz musicians become jazz musicians by learning from other experts. No one is born a jazz musician, it is a learned skill, but first, the musician must experience it by seeing an expert who has developed their skills at a higher level.

7. **Inspired by Aspirations**: Teach the difference between adoption and transformation. Aspire to transform the organization to be agile and not to do agile. Being a Jazz musician is not about doing jazz, one has to embrace and embody the philosophy of Jazz.

8. **Surrender to Support**: An agile transformation is a top-down decision that requires the organization's leadership to stand behind. All other team members must understand the organization vision for becoming agile and support the effort. Jazz musicians are consistently changing roles as one person solos and leads, and everyone else surrenders and supports the soloist. This creates a beautiful musical conversation between the musician, and they naturally understand that to make the music breath, they will sometimes lead, but will most often support the other musicians in the group.

9. **Excellence in Execution**: Establish a center of excellence where the top 10 to 20 percent of project managers will mentor and coach the rest of the teams. Make excellence the standard. Jazz musicians get better by seeking out and working with others who are much better than they are. This is the essence of growth and fulfillment as a Jazz musician. The goal of all great jazz musicians is not perfection, but excellence, and excellence can only be obtained from continuous growth from being around others who are better than you.

Assessment Questions

1. What was your first experience with music? How old were you, and what do you remember from the experience?

_____

_____

_____

2. What role does music play in your life now?

_____

_____

_____

3. How will your understanding of the neuroscience of music and its effects on brain development change your relationship with music and the role it will play in your life in the future?

_____

_____

_____

4. How can using the concepts and principles of music help you create a high-performing agile team?

_____

_____

_____

5. Can you describe the basic concepts, principles, and mindset for creating a workplace jazz environment?

_____

_____

_____

Additional Resources

- Art and science: how musical training shapes the brain (https://ncbi.nlm.nih.gov/pmc/articles/PMC3797461/)
- A Musical Approach to Agile Development Teams—Part 1 of 2 (https://resources.collab.net/blogs/a-musical-approach-to-agile-development-teams-part-1-of-2)
- Predictability over high-performance? My journey learning to play the guitar (https://leadingagile.com/2014/01/predictability-high-performance-journey-learning-play-guitar/)

CHAPTER 2

Improving Your Skills— Deliberate Practice

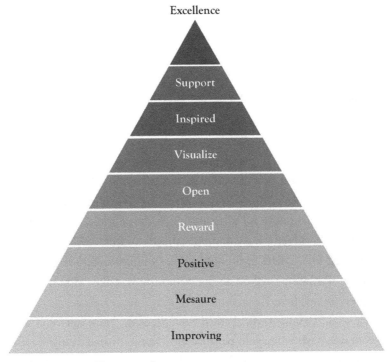

Workplace Jazz Framework

You can't use up creativity. The more you use, the more you have.
—Maya Angelou

Musicians don't retire; they stop when there's no more music in them.
—Louis Armstrong

When it comes to music, don't lie to yourself; just tell yourself the truth.
—Art Blakey

This chapter will teach you: you will be able to explain the what, why, and how of skill development like a jazz musician. The goal of all musicians is to develop the unconscious competence of their chosen instrument. Mastery is the ultimate goal of skill development on one's chosen instrument.

To play jazz at the highest level, the musician needs to learn their instrument like the back of their hand. They need to know it inside and out. During this chapter, we will look at examples of virtuoso musicians and how you can apply the same techniques to become an agile virtuoso.

Imagine this: You have spent many hours and years to earn your bachelor's degree in music, and you find yourself playing guitar in clubs and bars in Nashville.

This is how virtuoso guitarist and speaker Mike Rayburn developed his secrets to becoming the best in his field, one note at a time. Let us hear from Mike in his own words.

Mike: "In regards to practice and rehearsal and becoming your personal best, there are two decisions that changed my life. The first one happened in the late '90s. I had been playing the college market for a bunch of years. I had risen to pretty much the top of it. I was getting booked all the time. I was winning national awards, and my mentor, Brian Tracy, said, 'That's great, Mike. Have you resolved to be the best?' Meaning, like, what I call becoming virtuoso. I was like, 'Hey, man. I'm doing pretty well here.'"

He said, "That's not what I asked you." He said, "Have you resolved to be your best?" Meaning, your personal best, not compared to anyone else. And, I thought about it, and it knocked me over. The answer was, "No." Here I was, doing what I had been put on the planet to do and because it is working, I was coasting. It turns out most adults are coasting, and here is the problem with coasting. It only happens downhill.

"It was that day I made the decision to become my personal best. I call it, choose to become a virtuoso in whatever it is you do. It's kind of like, okay, what would you do? If you were going to become the best, what would you do? Would you read more? Would you practice more? Would you get a mentor? Would you have teachers regularly? Would you attend more concerts, attend more speaking events or whatever it is that you do?"

"I made a list. I came up with 11 things I could be working on, become my personal best. It was a line in the sand that day. And the success that would follow dwarfed anything I had done before, because I quit trying to rise to the level of just acceptable or successful or okay, and instead made a choice to rise to my personal best."

"The second decision was, as I was pursuing this, I would practice. I would put in the hours, and I know a lot of people who will practice. The problem is, they don't practice the right things. Anders Ericsson, I think, is his name, identified something called deliberate practice, meaning if I pick up a guitar and I just practice songs I know. I go over and over and over them again and play, I'm putting in the time, but I'm not actually moving forward. Instead, if I chart out a course for where I want to go, what I'm currently good at, but currently not good at, what I need to work on, where my weaknesses and mistakes are, and I rehearse those instead, I get more out of that time. That's deliberate practice."

"So, the two choices that changed my life were choosing to become a virtuoso and to practice like a virtuoso. And by the way, anyone can choose to become a virtuoso. What we find is the greatest impact, the greatest influence, the highest income happened between competent and virtuoso, along that path. And then the choice to practice deliberately, to work on the things that I'm not as good at, to get better within the medium of my expertise."

Mike Rayburn is an innovator. More importantly, as an entrepreneur, he has always turned innovation into profit. Mike has performed more than 5,000 presentations for thousands of organizations, including most of the Fortune 100. Mike has also headlined Carnegie Hall multiple times and shared the stage with the Beach Boys, Maroon 5, John Oates, and many other musical greats. To learn more about Mike Rayburn, go to https://mikerayburn.com/about/

How can you focus on developing your agile skills like a virtuoso guitarist?
All growth requires change.

Here are five steps to creating a high-performing agile project team and developing a mindset to improve your skills continuously:

The two choices that changed my life were choosing to become a virtuoso and to practice like a virtuoso. And by the way, anyone can choose to become a virtuoso.

Mike Rayburn

---

1. Remain vigilant and do your homework on trends, new developments, and your industry's value chain. What processes are being automated that will make you obsolete? What positions are being cannibalized by new technical developments or mobile applications? What roles are shipped to a global supply chain offshore? Are you prepared to move to where the value is as internal and external pressures modify the value chain?

2. Visualize yourself growing and mastering your skills. All virtuoso musicians and world-class athletes visualize. They do it because it works.

3. Get comfortable being uncomfortable. When you stretch yourselves to develop and move your skills to a new level, you will be uncomfortable, and growth requires stretching and doing something you are not familiar with. All growth requires change.

4. Take ownership of your skill development journey. To many of us who are waiting for our organizations to provide the necessary training and professional development, we will need to remain current. Although in the past, this was a great job benefit, it is no longer. We have to take 100 percent responsibility for our personal growth. Jazz musicians are responsible for their skill improvement, and everyone who plays understands that they are responsible.

5. Develop a love for lifelong learning, and do it for the value it will add to your life and not only an increase in pay. When you love what

you do and want to get better, you will work harder than you ever have, and you will love it because you are internally motivated by your desire for mastery.

Additionally, agile requires a team culture change, which most groups fail to achieve. To successfully change, the agile team must develop the skills to communicate effectively. Understanding the power of intentional conversations and the neuroscience of conversations intelligence can lay the foundation for creating positive transformational culture changes that work.

According to Judith E. Glaser, author of *Conversational Intelligence: How Great Leaders Build Trust and Get Extraordinary Results*, "To get to our next level of greatness depends on the quality of our culture, which depends on the quality of our relationships, which depends on the quality of our conversations ..."

"Everything happens through conversation!"

Ask yourself, when was the last time you attended a training program on how to conduct conversations effectively? The ability to communicate and affect a conversation has a direct impact on the release of positive or negative neurochemicals in your brain and in the brains of those we communicate with.

I didn't even start playing the piano until I was about 13 or 14. I guess I must have had a little talent or whatever-you-call-it, but I practiced regularly, and that's what counts.

—George Gershwin

Jazz musicians have to be on the same page when they perform. In the beginning, they spend time discussing their approach to how they will interpret the song for their performance. Others may play the same song with a different interpretation, and that is the beauty of jazz. This level of performance and interpretation requires deliberate practice. As Mike Rayburn is often quoted, "you have to practice deliberately to get better and become a virtuoso."

Success has to do with deliberate practice. The practice must be focused, determined, and in an environment where there's feedback.

—Malcolm Gladwell

How an opera singer I know uses the principles of deliberate practice.

Alice Dillon is an opera singer with the Washington National Opera and a music teacher in Maryland. Alice has two biblically based guiding principles that she uses in her career as a professional singer and teacher. The first one is that she always strives to be an excellent steward of her talent, and the second one is that if she has done her best, everything works out for the best.

As Alice told me, "Specifically, I can think of several examples where I auditioned for the Washington National Opera, and I thought I sang well. I felt like my voice was in good shape, but I didn't get a contract that year. However, there were several years when I did not get a contract, and I was able to have a solo gig somewhere else. Or I was able to either sing with the Strathmore Children's Chorus and Maryland Children's Youth Orchestra or one year I was able to sing as the soprano soloist for the Messiah sing-along at the Kennedy Center."

"So, other doors opened when one door closes. I can also think of times when I auditioned, and I felt like I had lost my voice or had become ill, or I had a memory slip. I would walk out of the audition, thinking, oh, that was terrible. That just didn't go the way I wanted, and then I would get the contract. So, I've come to believe that everything works out for the best if I've done my best that I can in the moment, as well as everything I can leading up to that moment."

"All this to say that I still get nervous, but I still prepare. I do everything I can to do my best, as much as it's up to me, and then it will work out. It always works out for the best, one way or the other."

As you are reading this, just remember that you must be the best you that you can be with the talents you have. *Prepare, study, and fine-tune your instrument or craft, and when you do, the opportunities and outcomes will eventually be the best ones for you.*

The Role of Deliberate Practice in the Acquisition of Expert Performance: "The differences between expert performers and normal adults are not immutable, that is, due to genetically prescribed talent. Instead, these differences reflect a life-long period of deliberate effort to improve performance."

—K. Anders Ericsson

An Old/New Approach to Practicing—Kata

Some jazz musicians have taken up martial arts, where they learned the concept of Kata. The famous jazz drummer Buddy Rich earned a black belt in Karate. "Kata is structured routines that you practice deliberately, especially at the beginning, so their pattern becomes a habit and leaves you with new abilities. Kata is a way of learning fundamental skills that you can build on. The word comes from the martial arts, where Kata is used to training combatants in fundamental moves."

The Neuroscience of Deliberate Practice

The deliberate practice embraces the concept of Kata. It involves attention, rehearsal, and repetition, which leads to new knowledge or skills that can later be developed into more complex knowledge and skills.

According to the American Psychological Association, "Deliberate practice occurs when an individual intentionally repeats an activity in order to improve performance. The Deliberate Practice framework claims that such behavior is necessary to achieve high levels of expert performance."

Dr. Jeffrey Schwartz, in his book *The Mind and The Brain*, references a study: "Robert Desimone of the National Institute of Mental Health, one of the country's leading researchers into the physiology of attention, explains it this way: Attention seems to work by biasing the brain circuit for the important stimuli." With deliberate practice, our brains naturally suppress distractions and improve focus.

How can you use the principles of deliberate practice to improve your agile management skills? According to the Society for Academic Emergency Medicine, in an article titled "Deliberate Practice and Acquisition of Expert Performance: A General Overview," by K. Anders Ericsson, PhD, states, "In direct contrast, aspiring experts continue to improve their performance as a function of more experience because it is coupled with *Deliberate Practice.*"

"The key challenge for aspiring expert performers is to avoid the arrested development associated with automaticity. These individuals purposefully counteract tendencies toward automaticity by actively setting new goals and higher performance standards, which require them to increase speed, accuracy, and control over their actions ... The experts deliberately construct and seek out training situations to attain desired goals that exceed their current level of reliable performance."

Without applying the rigor of deliberate practice to your skill development activities, you will plateau and limit your growth. The key to continuous improvement at any age for any skill is *deliberate practice.*

What skills do you need to develop to become an agile expert?

According to the editors at DICE.com, a technical job site for IT professionals, the top seven skills that agile team members should develop that will contribute the most to the creation of a high-performing agile team are:

- Business value
- Collaboration
- Confidence
- Product
- Self-improvement
- Supportive culture
- Technical excellence

Another way for teams to improve is to use the team self-assessment tool.

The Tabaka's team self-assessment model provides an additional level of rigor to assess the attributes for high-performing teams. Jean Tabaka developed the following high-performance team assessment, and you can learn more about her, and her work in the book *Collaboration Explained: Facilitation Skills for Software Project Leaders.*

Using the Principle of Deliberate Practice to Create a High-Performing Agile Project Team

Alignment exercise: First, team members write down 12 things that *agile* means to them and compare answers. In most cases, no two people will have the same answers, resulting in a misalignment around the core concept of what it means to be agile. Secondly, the team should spend time discussing the terms they captured and work together to develop an alignment on what agile means to the team.

Deliberate Practice Call to Action

To make the most of this chapter, complete the high-performing team self-assessment by going to https://principlesofexecution.nsvey.net/ns/n/ HighPerformingTeams.aspx.

Assessment Questions for Skill Mastery

1. What skills do you need to master to remain relevant in your role and to position yourself as an expert in your craft?

_____

_____

_____

2. How would imitating the deliberate practice process that jazz musicians use to improve skills and master their chosen instrument change the way you pursue skill development?

_____

_____

_____

3. Research and identify assessment tools that will help you identify your strengths and weaknesses. What resources did you discover? How can these tools enable you to target areas that you need to improve?

_____

_____

_____

4. How would you make a choice to become a virtuoso and to identify and practice the most critical skills to change your life as Mike Rayburn did?

_____

_____

_____

5. What are the top three skills you plan to master, and how will you implement the concept of deliberate practice to accomplish mastering them? Who or what will you seek out for mentoring, coaching, and consistent feedback on your journey of mastery?

_____

_____

_____

Additional Resources

- Becoming an expert takes more than practice: https://princeton. edu/news/2014/07/03/becoming-expert-takes-more-practice
- The Making of an Expert: https://hbr.org/2007/07/the-making-of-an-expert
- Deliberate practice for software developers: https://leadingagile.com/2018/09/deliberate-practice-for-software-developers/

CHAPTER 3

Measure What Matters

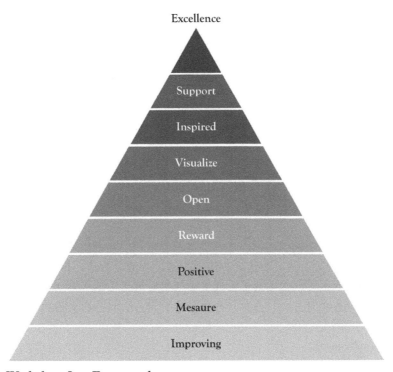

Workplace Jazz Framework

A jazz musician is a juggler who uses harmonies instead of oranges.
—Benny Green

It's taken me all my life to learn what not to play.
—Dizzy Gillespie

This chapter will teach you how to help your team develop collaborative goals and focus on delivering results that matter. To measure what matters first requires that you understand what matters most to your customers, leaders, and managers.

You must align your team's goals with the organization's goals. Think of goal alignment as a cascading waterfall. Come to think of it; musicians love waterfalls. Waterfalls create a rushing sound like the big bands of Count Basie or Duke Ellington, where the leader has a musical vision that is transferred to each musician in the group.

You will hear from David Snyder, a musician and business consultant who is a Harvard graduate and plays a mean guitar. We will then visit with a five-time Grammy-winning bassist, Victor Wooten, and his Bassology sidekick and collaborator Anthony Wellington.

We will round out this chapter reflecting on what we need to measure to become a high-performing agile team.

Now sit back and listen to the sounds of David Snyder as he shares one amazing night of hanging with friends that turned into a Brazilian jazz jam in Ottawa.

The "One Mind One Soul" Phenomenon of Jazz Bands—David Snyder

Picture this. Many moons ago, I was visiting Ottawa, Canada, and made my way into a large dance club with some friends. The place was packed, about a thousand people or more, and there was a Brazilian jazz band on stage with a flamenco guitar player, and other jazz players, backed by a killer percussion section made up of three conga players from Senegal.

I noticed an unused flamenco guitar sitting on stage on a stand. After the first set was over, I went up and asked the leader why there was an empty spot on stage and an unused guitar. He said the lead player was sick that night. I asked him if I could sit in with them for the rest of the night. He laughed at me and told me to go away.

I told him that I had been playing since I was 10 years old and he should give me a chance. So, he passed me the guitar from the stage and said, "Play something." "Okay," I said. And then, using four fingers on each hand, I did a lightning-fast Pepe Romero style riff in 32nd notes all the way from the 17th fret down to the open E string, hitting every string and half the notes on the guitar on the way down. He grinned and said in French, "Get up here."

I climbed on stage and played with them for two nonstop hours, during which the crowd went wild, and the dancing became wild and euphoric—we transported the crowd to another place. I had totally bonded with the conga players, and we were reading each other's minds— they were grinning at me, and I was laughing at them as we changed key signatures, tempos, and time signatures constantly over the course of two hours of nonstop music.

We never stop looking at one another. Once we hit our groove, it felt like we were the same entity, or soul, not really individual people, but just parts of the same collective thing.

It was surreal.

The women were screaming and dancing like crazy below, and so were the men. I felt like I was flying through space with a jetpack on, and the bandleader was smiling from ear to ear.

The crowd asked for about five encores, but at two in the morning, everyone was exhausted, so we had to stop. I never spoke a single word to anyone in the band from the moment I was handed the guitar, but we knew one another better than brothers by the time we were done.

Music—when it really cooks—is transcendent that way.

When the show was over, people came up to us, and one guy asked, "How do you guys do that? It is like you knew where the other person was going every second, but you have never met, never played together. How is that possible?"

The Senegalese guys just shrugged and laughed as if to say they had no answer.

But finally, in response to one of our new fan's persistent questions about improvisational skill—and where it comes from—I said:

Improvisation is all about listening—deep listening.

You sit in your room for 10 years practicing the guitar eight hours a day listening to records until your hands feel like they are going to fall off, and you learn how to listen. Really listen.

"Listening is an intense discipline. Listening is not about yourself. It is about other people. You learn how to listen to people's souls, and once you can do that, it becomes magic. You can connect with anyone anywhere. And you don't have to ask where they are going because you already know. At that level of listening, you are sharing the same mind."

Then, one of the Senegalese drummers said, smiling, "That's right. The same mind."

That night will forever stay in my mind; as years later, I am still mentoring musicians and songwriters and belong to many musical associations focused on improvisation and collaboration. I also own a few consulting businesses but have never left my musical roots—and I have people wandering in and out of my house and recording studio all of the time—a lot of really talented, beautiful people who also know how to listen extremely well. We have a lot of fun together.

Here is the moral to my story about that jazz club scene in Ottawa: In working with my business clients on leadership issues, I know beyond a shadow of a doubt that old-school approaches toward leadership, management, and performance management are dying—absolutely dying away.

An entirely new breed of team members is rising—especially in the technology world—and they are exactly like artists.

In this new teamwork-focused world, it is all about playing your instrument really, really well, and being able to listen and having tons of respect for the other artists around you, sharing the same mind. That is where true engagement comes from—deep listening, respect, playing well, mastering your instrument, and having fun as part of an orchestra, so to speak, even if your job is not a musical one. If you do not see that this change has occurred, you will be lost.

True engagement comes from—deep listening, respect, playing well, mastering your instrument, and having fun as part of an orchestra, so to speak, even if your job isn't a musical one.

Business is turning into jazz; it moves along the same path of improvisational, creative flow—a union of minds and souls. Because business and entrepreneurship have become so fluid and creative, an entirely new type of leadership is needed, one that sees the organization as a symphony of gifted players and not a roomful of worker bees. Those days are dead and buried. Anyone who cannot see that does not stand a chance.

David Snyder is an author, business consultant, book consultant, published researcher in psychology, Harvard graduate, composer, songwriter, producer, mentor to numerous independent artists, multi-instrumentalist, and virtuoso guitarist. He has released five albums in the last two years under his label, Day of Faith Records, and is currently working on a novel.

He is also ICAgile certified in software development and holds several patents, including a platform called Engagement View that provides robust analytics on employee engagement. His first book, *How to Mind-Read Your Customers*, is translated internationally and was listed first in best books of the year by the *Sales and Marketing Management* magazine the year of its release. His second book, *How to Hire a Champion*, has been used as a playbook for hiring and assessment by divisions of NBC and other major organizations. He can be found at www.mindread.net. And, he still practices his scales every day.

An entirely new type of leadership is needed, one that sees the organization as a symphony of gifted players and not a roomful of worker bees.

What was the goal of the Brazilian jazz band? Why did the band leader leave the lead guitar player on stage even though he was not available to perform? How important was it for each musician to know their instrument so well that they could generate a dancing environment that was wild and euphoric—and was able to transport the crowd to another place?

It all starts with first mastering your craft. Once you have mastered your instrument—be it coding, testing, managing, or leading—and are executing your skills at a high level, you are free to collaborate unselfishly. When musicians are competent in their skills, they can take the focus off of themselves and focus on listening and engaging with others.

In the same way, a high-performing agile team can operate in the zone because the individual members have embraced their instrument and skills with a focus on mastery. When they come together to solve a business problem, they can turn the focus to authentically listening and bringing out the best in each other. They have moved from a mindset of *I* to *we*.

The *problem* that teams face today, which keeps them performing at a lower level, is that they have not mastered their skills. So, when they come together, they have an *I*-focused mindset instead of a *we* or team mindset. They have not mastered the basics. In this way, when team members come together, they are full of insecurities and doubts.

Like jazz musicians, agile team members need to dedicate time alone to practice. They need to focus on mastery. Then, as each member becomes more proficient, they will become a high-performing team because they can turn their focus from themselves to the team.

By the way, trying to change too much at one time increases complexity and slows down the agile adoption and team transformation process. Members of the team should work on one thing at a time so that everyone can focus on getting better one step at a time.

Therefore, use an incremental approach to improving your agile team because people are more likely to accept small changes over time. Focus each incremental improvement on your core objectives and key results, which are also known as OKRs.

Improvisation is all about listening—deep listening.

OKRs (Objectives and Key Results) for Agile Teams

John Doerr, in his bestselling book *Measure What Matters*, popularized the concept of OKRs and defined it as, "A management methodology that helps to ensure that the company focuses efforts on the same important issues throughout the organization." So, the purpose of OKRs is to get everyone on the same sheet of music, playing the same song, and to create and execute harmoniously across the organization.

Jazz musicians have OKRs for each show they perform. They focus on a few objectives and their key priorities. Before a performance, jazz musicians will focus on play music that will engage and delight their audience. They want to help their fans forget about their troubles and get lost in the music—music that melts away their challenges, disappointments, and frustrations. They want to take their audience on a musical journey with them to experience the healing and spiritual power of music.

Most musicians focus on improving in three ways:

1. They are getting better on their chosen instrument with a passion for the art of mastery.
2. Engaging, listening, and connecting in a way that transcends their performance and musical moments. They sync up in a way that they know what the other musicians are thinking, feeling, and envisioning about the music without words. It is all about connecting on a much deeper level. Communicating with each other and the audience's soul.
3. And finally, delivering outstanding performance through supporting, collaborating, and expressing their love of music. Performing is about transmitting your passion and love for your art into the mind, soul, and spirit of the listeners. It is the reason you have to move when you hear your favorite band or song. You know, "Listen to that—they're playing my jam!" Remember.

This is why I chose the phrase "Measure What Matters" for the title of this chapter. Because once you have embarked on a journey of mastery, the only way to continuously improve is to measure your progress, individually and collectively, as a group.

To become a high-performing agile team, you have to measure your progress in the same way. You have to measure your progress individually, and you have to measure your progress as a team.

As an individual, you are tracking your improvement in your skills, how much code is being written, how many bugs are the testers finding in your code, and how many processes are being optimized. Progress is measured by your specific role in the project and how efficient and effective you are in contributing to the team.

As a team, you are measuring how the team is performing. How many user stories are being completed in each sprint? Are our customer satisfaction scores improving? Or, are we increasing the team velocity in completing the backlog requirements?

If you are interested in gaining a practical approach to using OKRs for a small team or a small business, here is a great article on the subject. I found it very useful in my research and when reviewing a technical solution to support the OKR process. The article is, "Getting Started with OKRs For Small Businesses": https://gtmhub.com/blog/getting-started-with-okrs-for-small-businesses/

By the way, in full disclosure, I am not a strategic partner with GtmHub; I found their content very helpful and easy to digest. So, if you decide to use their services, I will not receive payment for mentioning them in my book. Now that we have the legal stuff out of the way, let us continue.

One of the best ways to measure your progress and understand what matters is to consistently take an assessment of your team's progress on the key attributes or characteristics of a high-performing agile team. This can be done throughout the organization and for each team during the agile sprint reviews and retrospectives. In the scrum method of managing agile projects, the agile team along with the product owner, key business users, and technical managers perform a ceremony call the sprint review and retrospective. During these sessions, the team reviews what was accomplished during the previous sprint and reflects on what is working, what is not working, and what needs to be improved on the project.

The sprint review and retrospective is a perfect time to conduct an assessment that measures critical components of a high-performing agile team. This assessment can be leveraged to assess how your team is performing in the following areas:

- The degree of stakeholder's satisfaction and commitment.
- The team understand how the project is aligned with the business and that business value is being realized.
- Ability to deliver user stories and backlog items predictability through managing the work and schedule during each sprint reliably.
- Epics, features, users' stories, and tasks are decomposed to manage the scope realistically and in a controlled manner.
- Backlog refinement activities follow a standard and proven process that enables the team to be clear about their definition of *done* and agree on the acceptance criteria.

4. The team has high trust and respect for each other and is a high level of emotional intelligence.

- Individual team members take ownership and are accountable for their work.
- Risks are being mitigated through knowledge sharing and mindful reflection from team member experience.
- The delivery organization is excellent in learning, innovating, and continuous improvement.
- Costs and budgets are controlled through the team's self-governing accountability practices.
- A culture of excellence is visible through the agile process.

If you are wondering how your team is doing right now, then go to the following URL and have your team complete the workplace jazz high-performing agile team assessment now. That is right, do it now. This way, you will discover where your team is at on this high-performing agile team maturity curve. And, you will gain insight into how you can apply additional concepts I will cover throughout the rest of this book.

High-Performing Agile Team Assessment: https://principlesof-execution.nsvey.net/ns/n/HighPerformingTeams.aspx

It doesn't make sense to hire smart people and tell them what to do; we hire smart people so they can tell us what to do.

—Steve Jobs

Jazz is not just "Well, man, this is what I feel like playing." It's a very structured thing that comes down from a tradition and requires a lot of thought and study.

—Wynton Marsalis

Time isn't the main thing. It's the only thing.

—Miles Davis

Jack Canfield, Mark Victor Hansen, and Less Hewitt, in their book *The Power of Focus*, say, "Priority focus is all about setting new boundaries that you do not cross. First, you need to decide very clearly what those boundaries are, in the office and at home. Discuss these new parameters with the most important people in your life. They need to understand why you are making these improvements. You will also need their support to keep you on track. Most businesspeople get into trouble because they spend too much time on things they don't know much about. Stick to what you know best and keep refining these talents."

When changing your culture, you must narrow your focus on the activities that will produce the greatest return. You need to measure what matters and only what matters. You should recruit others to support your measuring efforts. Staying focused requires that you track your progress and monitor your activities within predictable intervals. Accountability is critical. So, partner with leaders who are not afraid to call you out and hold you accountable.

Modes of Rhythm: Victor Wooten and Anthony Wellington

I want to introduce you to a five-time Grammy-winning bassist and his sidekick, whom I met at a bass boot camp. When I thought about measuring what matters, their playing and teaching techniques on a YouTube video came to mind. They have an amazing way to teach younger bassists how to master the skill of keeping time. I want you to go to the You-Tube link and watch their video before you continue reading. I want you to watch this video—it is only about five minutes—and listen to how Anthony Wellington and Victor Wooten interact and teach modes of rhythm. For a bass player, having this technique and understanding the concept of modes of rhythm is what all great bassists must learn to be able to do to lay down a groove for any song, whether you are playing classical, jazz, funk, rock and roll, or bluegrass. As a bass player, we have to hold down the rhythm, and the way this ties into measuring what matters is they have developed a very detailed and sophisticated process for measuring the way you play rhythms so that you can master this skill.

Take a listen to the video, then when you are done, come back to this section to read the rest of this chapter: https://youtu.be/8Sw_trDFJw8. You will enjoy it.

To learn more about Victor Wooten and Anthony Wellington, go to https://victorwooten.com/ and http://bassology.net/.

Now you have had a chance to watch the video and listen to two amazing bass players who have for years traveled the world, astonishing people with their passion, sophistication, and funky bass playing. It fires me up when I listen to this video because they are taking the same concepts that we can use as an agile team working and teaching each other from our expertise and experience. Notice that they varied the rhythmic pattern and kept focusing on keeping time, and in the end, Victor starts giving more information about how to practice tracking time, which is critical to measure for bass players. Playing on time and in the groove is key for bassists. So, what are the key measures to track for an agile team? What areas should they focus on?

In his article "How Jazz Pianists Practice," Ted Rosenthal elaborates on the need to measure how you practice so that when you perform with the rest of the band, you are ready. He writes, "The jazz pianist is part pianist, part composer, and part arranger. In addition to 'traditional' pianistic skills, jazz pianists must also be able to improvise, harmonize melodies, instantly transpose, and create accompaniments in a variety of styles. They must also have highly developed rhythmic skills and be able to 'swing.' In a practice session, pianistic, as well as creative resources, need to be constantly challenged. Furthermore, the nature of performing in the jazz world often means little or no rehearsal time. The well-prepared jazz pianist must be ready for almost anything!"

Developing the Agile Mindset

The project team should develop a set of OKRs for their agile implementation by release or by feature set.

Information radiators can be used in developing an agile mindset because they facilitate information being available and visible for the entire team. For the whole team to see this information is critical and an important part of measuring what matters. Information radiators are the best way to remain aware of where the team is within the agile process and for managing a co-located or virtual team. An information radiator is a visual display of key information that the team needs to manage the overall agile project. Items that can be displayed on the information radiator may include features of the solution, delivery dates, and who is assigned to items to be worked on.

It could be a list of features or backlog items that are being worked on and what is currently being worked on within a sprint or an iteration if the team is tracking velocity, what is the velocity of each of the sprints, and what is the target velocity as well as the defect metrics.

You can also include information related to findings and items discussed in the retrospectives and sprint reviews, as well as tracking the project risk and issues. Alistair Cockburn initially created the term "information radiator."

Alistair wanted to resolve the issue of information being difficult to find or even hidden away. By creating a visual display, his coining of "information radiator," it made the critical information for agile teams available for everyone. These are perfect examples to use when striving to display things that you need to measure consistently.

Discovering Your Components to Measuring What Matters

Here is an exercise you can apply: work with your team's product owner and develop a set of OKRs for your project, agile implementation, process improvement, or department.

Then, use an incremental approach to implementing your team's agile OKRs. And, always remember, people can accept small changes over time; so, focus each increment on a limited number of core objectives and key results. Soon you will find your team vibing and grooving in the same direction.

Assessment Questions

1. Based on what you have learned in this chapter, what matters in your organization that your team needs to measure to become a high-performing team?

_____

_____

_____

2. How should you and your team go about assessing your ability to measure what matters? Should you develop your own set of OKRs or assessment categories, and how frequently should you take those measurements?

_____

_____

_____

3. What processes will you create to ensure that your assessments and lessons learned are implemented in continuous process improvement for your organization and your team so that you can become a high-performing agile team?

_____

_____

_____

4. What steps and training can you implement to make your team assessment capable or assessment ready?

_____

_____

_____

5. How can leveraging the high-performing agile team assessment consistently transform your team, and what additional areas should the assessment cover for your team specifically?

_____

_____

_____

Reference

John, D. 2018. *Measure What Matters: How Google, Bono, and the Gates Foundation Rock the World with OKRs*, 14. Penguin Publishing Group, Kindle Edition.

Additional Resources

- What Matters: https:/whatmatters.com/get-inspired/
- John Doerr on OKRs and measuring what matters: https:// sloanreview.mit.edu/video/john-doerr-on-okrs-and-measuring-what-matters/
- Measure What Really Matters: https://felipecastro.com/en/ blog/book-review-measure-what-matters/

CHAPTER 4

Cultivating Positive Attitudes

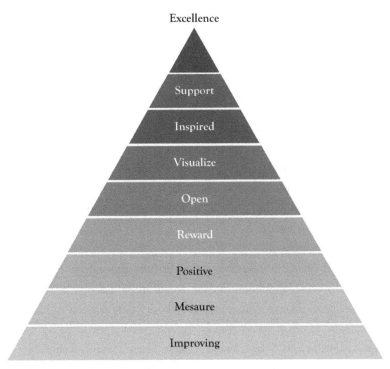

Workplace Jazz Framework

The place to start a positive attitude is with the little things. If you can learn to appreciate them and be grateful for them, you'll appreciate the big things as well as everything in between.

—John Maxwell

I want them to come away with discovering the music inside them. And not thinking about themselves as jazz musicians, but thinking about themselves as good human beings, striving to be a great person and maybe they'll become a great musician.

—Charlie Haden

This chapter will teach you how to analyze your stories, insights, and action steps to impact you and your team's personal attitude and the results you achieve.

You will learn how an opera singer transformed her passion from opera to be a folk singer and guitarist while starting her leadership communication training firm. She teaches a graduate-level public speaking course entitled "The Arts of Communication" at the Harvard Kennedy School. It all started with her attitude.

Next, we will visit the R&B Hall of Fame and award-winning jazz singer Phil Perry follows with a discussion on the latest neurological research on developing a positive attitude.

Finally, we round out our discussion on developing a positive agile mindset and the impact it can have on your team becoming a high-performing agile superpower within your organization.

What Do Opera, Folk Music, and Harvard Have in Common? The Answer: Allison Shapira!

Allison Shapira:

"Growing up, all I ever wanted to do was sing opera. I went to a performing arts high school, studied abroad in Italy, and went to college for vocal performance. But something about opera felt too distant, too inauthentic to me. It wasn't who I truly was—it was the role I felt others expected me to play. Disenchanted, I left opera and stopped singing.

But ten years later, I learned to play acoustic guitar, and everything changed. Through singing folk music, I actually found my authentic voice. I started writing and performing my music, and now I feel more alive and more genuine than I ever felt like an opera singer.

Opera always made me feel distant from people, while folk music makes me feel like we're on the same level.

I think real leadership is more like folk music than like opera. It's not about being the distant, perfect leader; it's about being inclusive and bringing others together so we can all sing the same song. That's how I teach people to give speeches, and that's how I encourage them to lead."

Allison Shapira is the CEO and founder of Global Public Speaking, a communication firm that trains to emerge and establishes leaders to speak with confidence and authenticity.

Allison works with global brands as a speaker, trainer, and executive communication coach. She also travels around the world with the non-profit Vital Voices Global Partnership, helping women leaders grow their business, run for office, or launch a nonprofit organization. She holds a master's degree in public administration from the Harvard Kennedy School, is a member of the National Speakers Association, and is an internationally renowned singer or songwriter who uses music as a way to help others find their voice and their courage to speak. She speaks Italian and Hebrew, has studied eight other languages, and has led programs on-site in Asia, Africa, Europe, the Middle East, and North and South America. She is the author of *Speak with Impact: How to Command the Room and Influence Others*, published by HarperCollins.

So, what is the problem with developing a positive attitude?

When our plans do not work out, as they initially did not for Allison, we can begin to doubt ourselves and our abilities. We start carrying around a backpack of doubt, which gets heavier and heavier, which causes us to worry and visualize a negative image of ourselves.

Imagine spending four years completing a degree in opera, only to realize that it is not where your passion lies. For most people, this type of setback would forever keep them from pursuing their dreams and place them on a path of living in fear. A path of being afraid of not being good enough, fearing that they have wasted their time, or being afraid to chase their dreams.

So, what is the problem with developing a positive attitude? It is simple; when we allow doubt, worry, and fear to consume our thoughts, we have no room to cultivate a positive attitude.

Here is another example of someone who could have allowed the ups and downs of life to consume them with doubt worry and fear, which would have kept them from being inducted into the R&B Hall of Fame.

Resistance to change is an attitude issue. Focus on developing change and transition management skills because most change happens at once, but transiting to the change takes time. Once a change happens, you must focus on transitioning to the change to make it the new normal.

If you have a positive attitude and constantly strive to give your best effort, eventually you will overcome your immediate problems and find you are ready for greater challenges.

—Pat Riley

Phil Perry's believability, passion, honesty, power, and positive attitude took him from singing backup to the R&B Hall of Fame.

Born on January 12, 1952, Phil Perry at 17 was discovered by a group of nuns in their Catholic Church when they heard him singing in the choir in East St. Louis. He went on to sing with the Montclairs from 1971 to 1975.

After the Montclairs disbanded, Phil moved to California to work as a singer and writer. He experienced several ups and downs, so we know he is human. During an interview, Phil shares that these ups and downs helped them to understand that God did not give him success quickly so that he would not lose it quickly. He needed to learn how to hold on to what he gained by working through his hardships.

Phil became a backup singer and sang for Johnny Mathis, Chaka Khan, Don Grusin, Dave Grusin, Freddie Herbert, Najee, Barbra Streisand, June Pointer, Fourplay, George Benson, and many other individuals and groups.

Phil shared the secret to what got him through the ups and downs of singing backup. He said, "I never looked at singing backup vocals as a step backward. I saw each performance as an opportunity to learn something. I tried to give my best effort to whoever thought enough of me to hire me to begin with, so I never looked at it as a step down. I looked at it as an opportunity to learn and add my voice to the creation of a song that they apparently couldn't do by themselves; otherwise, they would not have called me."

When Perry referred to his style, he said that his style of singing was believability, passion, honesty, power, and tenderness. On his journey, he has produced over 10 solo albums, with many awards and was inducted into the R&B Hall of Fame in 2019.

You can still hear Phil singing with passion and power at https://philperrymusic.com/.

So, what was the cornerstone that enabled Phil Perry to have a productive and passionate career for the past five decades? What kept him smiling and believing in himself and his abilities? Why were so many brand-name singers, artists, and bands looking to hire Phil and add his voice to their recordings in a way that no one else could?

I believe it was his positive attitude, and as Phil said himself, "it was my believability in me."

To develop a high-performing team, its foundation must be a positive attitude, and its believability and passion for its purpose.

What are the benefits of developing a positive attitude?

According to Johns Hopkins Medical Center, "People with a family history of heart disease who also had a positive outlook were one-third less likely to have a heart attack or other cardiovascular event within five to 25 years than those with a more negative outlook." That is the finding from Johns Hopkins expert Lisa R. Yanek, M.P.H., and her colleagues.

So, not only can a positive attitude help you build a high-performing team, it could save your life!

Here are a few benefits of a positive attitude I have discovered:

- Increased productivity: People love working with a person with a positive attitude. Do you find yourself saying "no problem" or "it's my pleasure?" The latter is a positive reply.
- People with a positive attitude have a stronger immune system and get sick less often.
- A positive attitude helps you weather the storms of life and bring more joy to your journey.
- People with a positive attitude have more energy.
- A positive attitude reduces stress and the impact of cortisol and adrenaline on your body.
- People with a positive attitude are presented with better opportunities because people like to work with them.
- It will improve your team's ability to get things done and work through difficult problems.
- It helps leadership teams make better decisions.
- And, it helps you become a member of a high-performing team.

So, not only can a positive attitude help you build a high-performing team, it could save your life!

The Neuroscience of Positive Attitudes

In an *Inc.* magazine article titled "New Stanford Study: A Positive Attitude Literally Makes Your Brain Work Better," researchers discovered that a positive attitude literally changes your brain.

"To start to tease this out, a research team out of Stanford recently analyzed the math skills and attitudes of 240 kids aged seven to ten, as well as running 47 of them through an fMRI machine while asking them to do some basic arithmetic. What did they find?"

"As expected, kids who did well in math liked math more, both according to self-reports and their parents, and kids who hated the subject did poorly. But the brain scans also turned up something much more fascinating. The images revealed that the hippocampus, a brain area linked with memory and learning, was significantly more active in kids with a positive attitude toward math."

"'Attitude is really important,' said Chen. 'Based on our data, the unique contribution of positive attitude to math achievement is as large as the contribution from IQ.'"

Musicians are impacted by developing a positive attitude when they are performing by the process of mirror neurons, which activates when they work together. When a musician sees another musician overcome a musical challenge, they are more likely to feel confident that they can overcome it as well. Jazz musicians tend to imitate each other during the performance; this is all based on the mirror neuron effect.

Are you building a better brain with your team by cultivating a positive attitude? The research is in, and now it is your turn.

Eight Steps for Creating a High-Performance Positive Attitude

1. Develop a clear vision for the type of culture and character you want in your team. By creating a vision of where you are going and the type of team that is going to be needed to get there, you will generate a picture in the minds of your team members so that everyone individually can visualize who they need to become and where they need to be to make your dreams come true.

2. Take 100 percent responsibility for the attitude of your team. When everyone on the team takes 100 percent responsibility for their attitude and their outlook, the team will generate an atmosphere of camaraderie and collaboration. Work will become a place where team members love to be and want to hang out.

3. Establish your team's rules of engagement. By establishing rules of engagement, you are setting boundaries on how meetings, ceremonies, sprint reviews, retrospectives, and any other type of team meeting will be conducted. When everyone understands what to expect at a team meeting, they will arrive more prepared and ready to give and collaborate.

4. Define your team's values together. Values are simply behaviors that govern how we work together. So, by establishing a set of values and prioritizing those values for the team, everyone has the criteria on which they can act.

5. Generate buy-in from each member of the team so that everyone is on the same page and marching in the same direction. It takes a team to win the Super Bowl or the World Series, and it will take a group of dedicated individuals to develop a high-performing team. Everyone on the team must buy into the vision, the values, and the direction, and take 100 percent responsibility for the team's attitude. As I stated in my previous book, *Culture Is the Bass*, "buying is a team sport."

6. Set an example and remember the mirror neuron effect. When the leader sets the example, everyone has something to model their behavior against, so if the leader's attitude is positive, then by the

principle of mirror neurons, they will begin to model and imitate the leader's behavior.

7. Establish a cadence of accountability and team rituals. When everyone is holding each other accountable under a collective agreement, then everyone wins. Because it is no longer the leader holding the team accountable, but the team is holding each other and the leader accountable.

8. Create moments of celebration. Finally, take time to celebrate regularly. This will release neurotransmitters—brain chemicals in everyone on the team. This will generate a great feeling in a positive reaction. When teams take time to celebrate victories or small or large achievements, they are individually and collectively releasing chemicals such as dopamine, serotonin, and GABA into their brains, which will generate a positive experience and help establish a positive attitude.

The Positive Agile Mindset

Following are copies of the Agile Manifesto and the 12 principles of the Agile Manifesto. When you review these documents and read the principles behind the manifesto, imagine attempting to implement these principles and values with the negative or disengaged mindset.

Being successful as a high-performing agile team requires the development of a positive attitude. If you study the stories and the principles I have outlined earlier in his chapter, they will help you to develop a positive attitude so that you and your team strive to develop the mindset of an agilest. We all have the basic neurological foundation to put these principles to enter practice in our environment.

The Agile Manifesto

We are uncovering better ways of developing software by doing it and helping others do it. Through this work, we have come to value:

- Individuals and interactions over processes and tools
- Working software over comprehensive documentation
- Customer collaboration over contract negotiation
- Responding to change over following a plan

That is, while there is value in the items on the right, we value the items on the left more.

The 12 principles are based on the Agile Manifesto.

1. Our highest priority is to satisfy the customer through early and continuous delivery of valuable software.
2. Welcome changing requirements, even late in development. Agile processes harness change for the customer's competitive advantage.
3. Deliver working software frequently, from a couple of weeks to a couple of months, with a preference to the shorter timescale.
4. Business people and developers must work together daily throughout the project.
5. Build projects around motivated individuals. Give them the environment and support they need and trust them to get the job done.
6. The most efficient and effective method of conveying information to and within a development team is face-to-face conversation.
7. Working software is the primary measure of progress.
8. Agile processes promote sustainable development. The sponsors, developers, and users should be able to maintain a constant pace indefinitely.
9. Continuous attention to technical excellence and good design enhances agility.
10. Simplicity—the art of maximizing the amount of work not done—is essential.
11. The best architectures, requirements, and designs emerge from self-organizing teams.
12. At regular intervals, the team reflects on how to become more effective, then tunes and adjusts its behavior accordingly.

Assessment Questions

1. What have you learned in this chapter that can help you and your team develop a positive attitude?

_____

_____

_____

2. How will you and your team go about evaluating your vision, values, and rituals to ensure you have a process and a framework to reinforce the development of your team's positive attitudes?

_____

_____

_____

3. What steps could you add to the eight-step process for developing a positive attitude?

_____

_____

_____

4. What do Allison and Phil's story have in common that helped them to persevere through life's ups and downs?

_____

_____

_____

5. How can you use the principle of mirror neurons to influence your organization to develop a positive attitude?

_____

_____

_____

Additional Resources

- How to select and develop individuals for successful agile teams: https://scrumorg-website-prod.s3.amazonaws.com/drupal/2019-01/How-to-select-individuals-for-agile-teams-vFinal.pdf
- Positive Intelligence: https://hbr.org/2012/01/positive-intelligence
- How to Create a Positive Attitude: https://inc.com/geoffrey-james/how-to-create-a-positive-attitude.html

CHAPTER 5

From Risk to Reward

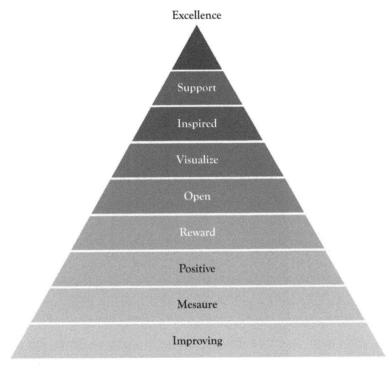

Excellence

Support

Inspired

Visualize

Open

Reward

Positive

Mesaure

Improving

Workplace Jazz Framework

When you hit a wrong note, it's the next note that makes it good or bad.

—Miles Davis

A lot of people approach risk as if it's the enemy when it is fortune's accomplice. A risk you take may seem ridiculous to other people, but the risk isn't random or rash when it's a necessity.

—Sting

This chapter will teach you how to describe how a lack of risk management will impact your personal and team performance and how, with a few simple techniques, you will be able to mitigate your risk and capture your desired rewards.

We will hear from the Hall of Fame speaker, talented guitarist, and customer service expert Shep Hyken on how capturing your rewards comes from taking some risk.

You will meet George Whitty, virtuoso jazz pianist and teacher at Artist Works, and his insight on managing performance risk.

We will discuss how managing risk affects our brains and how we can use this knowledge to our advantage. I will share a tool I developed to manage risk on my agile projects I called the risk burndown chart.

Finally, I will introduce you to a risk management and lesson learned strategy I have used following the *LEARN model*, which I learned from Judith Glaser, author of conversational intelligence.

Shep Hyken: There's No Reward Without Taking Some Risk ...

Shep Hyken here. Growing up, I started playing guitar when I was 12 years old. I also started doing magic tricks when I was about 10 or so. I started doing performances at about age 12, and one thing I learned very quickly is that I was nervous. I would get in front of an audience, whether it be to do a magic show or to perform music, and I would be nervous—so nervous, in fact, that I would shake. It didn't matter if it was a birthday party, and I was doing magic shows for six-year-old kids, or I was performing guitar in my jazz band at school in front of a larger audience. But this is what I learned. Every time I put myself out there in front of an audience and I pushed myself to either try something new, do new material, or just push myself when I felt like I'm uncomfortable, I always ended up being better in the long run. The payoff was that I pushed myself to a point but found that that was really within my comfort zone ultimately.

So, the moral of this story, if you will, is that the further I pushed myself, the better I became. Whether it be a magic show, and I'll never forget doing magic shows in my teenage years for audiences and shaking, I was so scared, or performing in my band. I remember being 16 years old stepping out on stage in front of 400 people playing hard jazz, actually a Bossa Nova jazz song, Antonio Carlos Jobin's one-note samba, which by the way isn't just one note, or "Girl from Ipanema," and I'm out there playing the lead, playing the head, and I'm shaken, but I'm performing. And you know what? Every time I did it, I became better for it.

In recent years I performed in front of thousands of people playing guitar, but the key was, as nervous as I was getting up, and maybe it's just anticipation and excitement the key to being successful was that I was always prepared. I always rehearsed, maybe even over-rehearsed, because when I got out there, there was one thing I was never nervous about. I was never nervous about not knowing my material. I was never nervous about not knowing what key I was supposed to play in, what hook I was supposed to play when I was supposed to take the lead.

Put yourself out there. Push yourself. You'll be better for it in the long run. And most importantly, when you get out there, be prepared. Because the one place you don't want to be nervous, the one place you don't want to have any concern over whether or not you know your material is when the curtain opens and the spotlight is on you.

Shep Hyken is a customer service and experience expert and the *Chief Amazement Officer* of Shepard Presentations. He is a *New York Times* and *Wall Street Journal* bestselling author of *Moments of Magic, The Loyal Customer, The Cult of the Customer, The Amazement Revolution*, and *Amaze Every Customer Every Time.*

Shep works with companies and organizations that want to build loyal relationships with their customers and employees. His articles have been read in hundreds of publications. He is also the creator of The Customer Focus™, a customer service training program that helps clients develop a customer service culture and loyalty mindset.

To learn more about Shep Hyken, go to https://hyken.com/

But, what if I work in an environment that has unrealistic expectations for my team and me? Wow, I am so glad you asked that question, and we are on the same page.

Does your boss have an unrealistic expectation? Mine did.

Merriam-Webster defines expectations as the act or state of expecting; anticipation. So, then, unrealistic expectations are having the wrong ideas that things will be accomplished or take place, but without any factual evidence.

In other words, unrealistic expectations are someone's vision of the future that is made up and based on their thoughts, desires, and fantasies.

I am sure somewhere in your past—definitely in mine—you have come across or had to work with a manager or a boss who had unrealistic expectations. What I have learned is that unrealistic expectations are the result of what neural scientists call an amygdala hijack. And, amygdala hijack happens when we become overwhelmed and paralyzed by fear.

We start making unrealistic assumptions for ourselves and for others. It is being controlled by fear, worry, and doubts, so we try to push or force our will, opinions, and thoughts on others to accomplish what we want, but what we want is not based in reality. This can cause undue stress for everyone ... all around the organization. Yes, even your boss is stressed!

The next time you find yourself working with someone who has an unrealistic expectation and is experiencing an amygdala hijack, try these five steps, which can help you cope in an unrealistic workplace environment:

Five Steps to Managing Unrealistic Expectations

1. Manage your stress responses: When we are in an environment controlled by unrealistic expectations, our bodies start producing cortisol and adrenaline; it is part of the fight or flight syndrome. These are neurotransmitters that our bodies produce when we feel threatened. As we are no longer being chased by sabretooth tigers, or in fear of being eaten by a mountain lion, we need to calm ourselves and take control of our thoughts and bodies. And, by thinking rationally and taking a few deep breaths, we can reverse the flow of these neurotransmitters and bring our stress levels under control.

2. Find common ground: When you are presented with an unrealistic expectation, somewhere in those expectations are common ground activities that you and your boss or manager can agree upon. In my book *Culture Is the Bass*, I shared a story I called 15 Days Till Liftoff. It is based on a situation where a new team was brought together. I was assigned as the lead consultant, and we had 15 days to complete a proof of concept of two enterprise systems that we needed to integrate. However, nothing had been ordered or installed, and the team had never worked together. My first job was to calm myself and find common ground with the executive making the request. We were

able to work together as a team and deliver the proof of concept on day 14, coming in one day early. And, we did it by finding common ground, calming ourselves, and working with the executive to meet his objective.

3. Identify quick wins: Whenever you are faced with an unrealistic expectation, one of the ways to buy yourself and your team some time is to identify within those common grounds a few quick wins. Quick wins are items or tasks that can be done quickly. They show that the team is making progress and gives the executive confidence that we are taking his or her request seriously. Delivering on a quick win will normally calm down unrealistic expectations and buy the team some additional time.

4. In order to quill the amygdala hijack effects, develop a detailed action plan. Provide a detailed action plan with dates and times for task completion. This action plan will also show the big picture roadmap and provide confidence that things can get done. The detailed action plan gives the executive something concrete to hold onto, based on realistic expectations.

5. Invite them to a daily standup meeting: one of the best ways to show an executive or manager how the team is progressing toward their expectations is to invite them to your daily standup. Let them know that a daily standup meeting is only a 15-minute meeting, where everyone stands up and gives their status. The team quickly discusses what was accomplished, what work is planned to be accomplished today, and if there are any impediments. That is it. The team is getting work done on the action plan and keeping things moving forward. By participating in daily standup, the executive will see and hear firsthand the effort and progress the team is making.

If you're not making a mistake, it's a mistake.

—Miles Davis

Music is your own experience, your thoughts, your wisdom. If you don't live it, it won't come out of your horn. They teach you there are boundary lines in music. But man, there's no boundary line to art.

—Charlie Parker

The beautiful thing about learning is that nobody can take it away from you.

—B.B. King

George Whitty, virtuoso jazz pianist—risks taking the lead to his high-performing secrets

George Whitty grew up in a little fishing town in Oregon where you would not hear jazz played on the local radio, whatsoever. He developed an interest in learning to play the piano early in life, so his parents found a few older ladies, who at that time wore bonnets, who provided him with a solid foundation in the fundamentals of good piano technique.

He was exposed to classical and traditional piano during the next 10 years. However, classical music was not his thing. Still, he did like the music of Rachmaninoff and Debussy, but not the powdered wig-wearing type of classical music of Mozart and Beethoven.

If you are old enough, do you remember that Columbia Records would send you so many records for free for joining their record club? Well, while in high school, George signed up for the Columbia record offer. Each month they would send him a record, and if you recall, you would have a choice in what they sent you. So, one of the records he received was a Captain & Tennille album. And, in this recording package was an offer for *Keyboard* magazine. George jumped on the offer for the magazine.

It was in *Keyboard* that he discovered jazz pianist Chick Corea. From falling in love with the jazz piano of Chick, George decided to investigate the history of jazz piano and fell in love with the music of Bud Powell and Art Tatum. By the time he was ready to head off to college, he was a solid bebop jazz pianist.

He applied to Berkeley College of Music. His parents did not want to tell him that he could not pursue his dreams, but, coming from a fishing and lumber town in Oregon, they could not envision their boy growing up to be a jazz pianist. Can you imagine? What would the neighbors think?

They agreed to allow him to go, but would only give him tuition for two years of study. George jumped at the opportunity. He was not going to learn to play jazz in the fishing and lumber town of Oregon. So, he headed off to Boston, where he studied for two years. When the two years were up, and the tuition ran out, he and a friend headed to New York City to pursue his dream of being a jazz pianist with 100 U.S. dollars in his pocket. Talk about taking a chance; he moved to Brooklyn.

In Brooklyn, he and his friend met and connected with some local musicians that they knew and shared an apartment. In those days, that was the only way to make it in New York City with the price of rent. He spent several years in the trenches working various gigs in New York.

During this time, a fellow studio musician came to him with a problem. He had been hired to write a song and create a demo for Celine Dion, and it was not going well. The friend asked George if he would mind taking a whack at it and see what he could come up with. George rearranged the song and recorded a demo of what he created.

When the producer received the demo from George, he was contractually obligated to play it for Celine, and she loved it. According to an interview George gave on "Jazz-Rock TV" on YouTube, he said that when Celine heard the song, she said, "I like that just the way it is." The song was "Falling Into You," which Celine recorded in 1996.

After the Celine Dion recording, George was introduced to Chaka Khan, which launched his recording and producing career.

George developed into a world-class musician, producer, composer, music engineer, and teacher. He won an Emmy Award as a composer for the TV show *All My Children*. Although he grew up in rural America, he was willing to step out and risk failure to make his dream of becoming a jazz pianist come true. He later had to take a bigger risk with moving to Brooklyn, New York, with 100 U.S. dollars in his pocket, to become the working jazz musician he dreamt of becoming.

George has performed with Grover Washington Jr., The Brecker Brothers, Chaka Khan, Richard Bona, Carlos Santana, and Celine Dion. He has produced over 100 CDs and has created hundreds of compositions for TV and film.

According to his website, he has also performed with Herbie Hancock, Wayne Shorter, Marcus Miller, Dave Holland, and Zakir Hussain in a concert for peace at the Hollywood Bowl.

George Whitty's career is the touchstone for the saying "No risk, no reward."

To a certain extent, a little blindness is necessary when you undertake a risk.

—Bill Gates

Every practice, rehearsal, or performance is an opportunity to learn and grow as a jazz musician when they are consistently reviewing what is working and what is not working.

Success or failure in business is caused more by the mental attitude even than by mental capacities.

—Walter Scott

Why is risk management essential to developing a high-performing team?

According to the *Harvard Business Review* article "3 Reasons You Underestimate Risk," there are three blind spots we all have when it comes to managing risks:

1. We get caught up in the reward, which can obscure our vision of potential risks. Our success can be the greatest lever to our downfall. We get caught up and forget to plan for future issues.
2. We forget about the sunk cost of bad investments. In a study conducted by the National Institute of Health, they discovered that once we invest in a project or solution and it is no longer working the way we expected, we have a neurological maker that is linked to the episodic memory that makes us blind to our losses. It is basically "the inclination to resist an action after previously bypassing a similar action." In other words, we get stuck in our ways and do not want to change or adjust our actions.
3. Finally, we become blind because of something known as *future aversion*. According to Srini Pillay MD, "the problem of assuming that the future, if unknown it cannot be tested." In other words, we wing it. We are willing to take our chances. We do not have the data, and it is too hard to get. So, we wing it.

The risk management process can help you and your team to avoid these blind spots.

As a member of a high-performing agile team, you can prevent this by developing a mitigation plan for those blind spots and schedule a risk review and assessment during each sprint review and retrospective in your projects.

In our earlier examples, both Shep and George took risks to fulfill their dreams. But, they also took steps to count the cost and plan for unknown risks, whether it was developing a 10-year plan, as Shep did, or moving in with roommates in Brooklyn who also were musicians, as George did. We all need to manage our risks and plan for unknown events.

We have to develop a risk management plan based on a set of best practices that are repeatable and predictable.

Here is an example of the PMI Risk Management Framework that you can use with your team to perform your risk assessments and develop a risk response plan in the event a risk rears its ugly head on your project.

The Agile Mindset

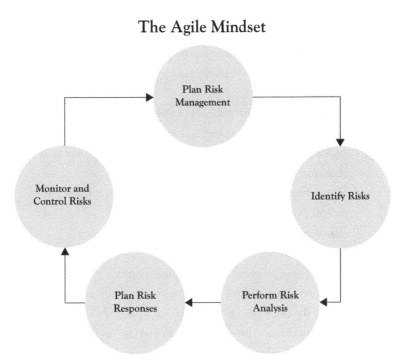

Figure 5.1 Risk Management Process

The following is my rendition of managing risks using the PMI process as a framework.

- Identify
  - Brainstorm ideas to identify potential risk, risk responses, and risk mitigation strategies.
  - You and your team should identify the level of exposure that each risk could have on your project.
  - You will also discuss as a team each risk's impact on the requirements of the project.
  - Identify potential cost and schedule impacts of the risk you have identified.
  - Finally, identify the various categories each risk should be organized into.
- Qualitative and quantitative analysis
  - During this step, the team should qualify each risk by thinking through the probability and impact each risk will have. It is color-coding the risk as high, medium, or low. High equals red, medium equals yellow, and low equals green. This can be facilitated using a probability impact matrix.
  - For quantifying your risk, according to the article "How to link the qualitative and the quantitative risk assessment," by Paolo Rossi. He says that "the quantitative approach requires:
  - The definition of the probabilistic value of each single risk factors occurrence, and
  - The quantitative definition of the potential impact."
- Response planning
  - The response planning process requires that the team determines how each risk will be mitigated and what events will trigger the risk so that everyone knows when the risk event is likely to occur. There are four ways you can respond to a negative risk. They avoid, mitigate, transfer, or accept. There are also four ways to respond if a risk is positive (i.e., too many downloads of your software that crashes the system; this is a

positive risk because a lot of people want your product, but the risk is that your current system cannot handle the increased demand); they are exploited, enhance, share, or accept. Other books on project management, like the project management body of knowledge, go into great detail about each of these risk responses, so I would refer you to them if you want to learn more about positive or negative risk responses.

- Response implementation
  - During this step, you will act on the detailed action plans or mitigation strategies you have developed with your team for each risk you have identified.
- Monitoring
  - Monitoring is the ability to watch, track, and evaluate the effectiveness of your risk management process throughout the project by having risk reviews during each agile sprint review and retrospective.

Another framework that can be used when discussing risk is the LEARN model. Take the retrospective review session to a deeper level to ingrain the learning for the team.

Exercise: Lessons learn using the LEARN model (Judith Glaser—Conversational Intelligence)

What did you like?

What did you expect?

What are you anxious about?

What should we reframe, focus, or direct?

What do you need?

Assessment Questions

1. What have you learned in this chapter that can help you and your team better manage risks and develop a risk management strategy on your projects?

_____

_____

_____

2. How will you and your team go about using the insight about risks management you have gained in this chapter?

_____

_____

_____

3. What steps will you take to implement a risk management strategy on your current and future projects?

_____

_____

_____

4. What does Shep and George's story have in common that helped them to manage risks as they pursued their dreams and goals through their life's ups and downs?

_____

_____

_____

5. How can you use the risk burndown chart to help you and your team identify, plan, analyze, implement, track, and monitor your risk response strategy throughout your project?

_____

_____

_____

Additional Resources

- Risk Management in Agile Projects: https://isaca.org/resources/isaca-journal/issues/2016/volume-2/risk-management-in-agile-projects
- No-Risk, No Reward: https://fastcompany.com/44778/no-risk-no-reward
- 3 Reasons You Underestimate Risk: https://hbr.org/2014/07/3-reasons-you-underestimate-risk

CHAPTER 6

Open to Feedback

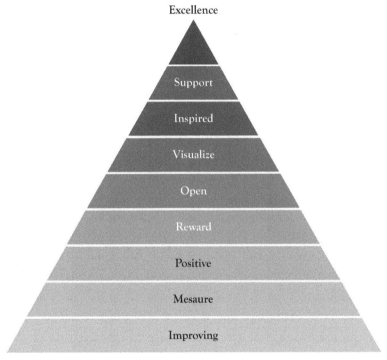

Workplace Jazz Framework

Feedback is the breakfast of champions.

—Ken Blanchard

This chapter will teach you the importance of being open to feedback. Being open to feedback requires having a growth mindset and continuously looking to improve.

On our first stop, we will hear from Bruce Turkel. Besides being a talking head on CNN, MSNBC, ABC, CBS, and FOX Business as a Branding and Marketing Expert, Bruce also plays a mean harmonica.

Next, we will ponder the concept of why do we avoid feedback.

We will also pick up some ideas about going after feedback from jazz musician Chuck Loeb, guitarist from the band FourPlay.

Our journey will then take us to review the benefits of feedback, steps we can take to fall in love with feedback, and finally, how we can leverage feedback to build a high-performing agile team.

Are you ready? ...

Bruce Turkel—a branding and marketing expert who plays a mean harmonica

There was this song we worked on in the band that I was in for years and years. Every single weekend, we would practice Saturdays. We always practiced on Saturday afternoons, and we would rehearse the song called "Too Tall to Mambo." It is a song by the Nighthawks. And, we rehearsed it week after week after week, but we never played it out. And, every couple of weeks when we were out, I would say to Chris, who is our lead singer, our lead guitar player, and really the head of the band. I would say, hey Chris, why do not we do "Too Tall to Mambo," and he would always say no.

So, one night we were playing somewhere, it was the end of our set, we had one song left, and I said to Chris "hey, why don't we do 'Too Tall to Mumbo'?" And, he said "no," and I said, "You know what, Chris? I don't understand. We rehearsed this song week after week after week, and we never play it. I don't get it; it's a great song. Why don't we do it?" So, he looks at me, and he says, fine, you want to play it, you sing it.

Now I got to tell you, I am not the singer in the band, and I even had throat surgery, so at the time, my voice was not in particularly good shape, but I wanted to do the song, so I said fine, I would do the song. So, I moved up front; I make a little announcement. "Hey, y'all, we're going to do a new song we've been working on for years, we've got it ready for you, we hope you dig it. It's our last song of the night, here we go."

I call the song off, and we start playing, and of course, we knew it because we rehearsed it all the time. I knew the words, I sang it, it was in a key I could handle. I guess I did an okay job, but in the middle of the refrain, the refrain is quite simply "Too Tall a Mambo," she's too tall to Mambo, and you just repeat it over and over. So, after doing it a couple of times, I told the band to quiet down, you know. I made a little hand signal—"hey, come on, band, hey y'all bring it down," and I said to the audience: Look at the last song of the night. Who wants to be a rock star? And, a couple of people put their hands up, and I said, "you, you, and you, these three girls, why don't you come up and sing with us?" Chris, the guitar player, is looking at me like I am out of my mind, but I bring the three girls up, I have them introduce themselves, and I say, "okay, here's the way it works. I'm going to sing 'Too Tall to Mambo,' and then you all sing 'Too Tall to Mambo.' And look, it's only four words, Too Tall to Mambo, and when you stop and think about it, *too* and *to* is the same word, so it's only three words. Not very much to learn—let's do it."

So, I sing "She's too tall to Mambo," and then I point to the three girls, you sing, and they go "too tall the mambo." I sing "too tall," and we go around twice, then I get the audience singing, and then I call the band back in, and we do it, we do the bridge, we do the verse, we do a couple of choruses—boom, we are out. Thank you all very much. We are the Rabble Rousers, here is Chris, our fearless leader, and hey, we had a great time. Thank you, good night, and we stop playing.

A few minutes later, you know, people are applauding. They are having a great time. They come up to talk to us. I go looking for Chris—I cannot find him. I look all over the bar. I cannot find him. Finally, I walk outside, and he is sitting outside drinking a beer, and he is pissed. I could just tell by his body language. So, I say to him, "Chris, wasn't that great? That song went great. I'm so glad we did it." He just looks at me angrily, and I say, "What's wrong? What's wrong? It's great, we did a great job, and they loved it."

He says to me, "You know, I want to be a professional musician; I want to make it as a musician. When I sing, nobody listens, nobody pays attention, nobody cares." He says, "You can't even freaking sing, and you sang that song and people were dancing, and people were on stage, and they applauded. We got a standing ovation. It's not fair. We give them good music, and they don't even care."

I said, "You know what Chris, if they wanted to hear good music they would stay home, put on headphones, and listen to Leonard Bernstein conduct the New York Philharmonic, doing Tchaikovsky. That's not why they come out. They come out to have fun; they come out to have a good time; they come out to be somebody."

Like I always say, in brand building, a good brand makes you feel good, but a great brand makes you feel good about yourself. We made them feel good about themselves; we got those three girls up on stage. They were happy, their friends were happy, their boyfriends were happy, the waitresses were happy because they got bigger tips. We got everybody dancing; they had a good time.

The point of rock 'n' roll music is to procreate the species. If these people go home and spend time together, we did our job. Agility in execution, what was it all about? We executed not a virtuoso performance, but we entertained our audience; we executed in an entertaining matter. We were agile to try something new, and we changed the evening for the participants, for the band, and for the bar.

They call us back all the time now, and "Too Tall to Mambo" has become our trademark song, and it was all because we changed the definition of what we were doing from creating good music to entertaining people. We did it with execution and agility.

Bruce Turkel has helped create some of the world's most compelling brands, including Miami. Bruce has worked with Hasbro, Nike, American Express, Charles Schwab, Citicorp, Discovery Networks, Bacardi, Sol Melia Hotels, Azamara Club Cruises, and many more great companies.

The highest-paid people in the world love feedback.

A captivating speaker and author, Bruce, has spoken at MIT, Harvard, TEDx, and hundreds of corporate and industry conferences. Bruce appears regularly on FOX Business and has been on CNN, ABC, CBS, and NPR. He has been featured in *The New York Times*, *Fast Company*, *Communication Arts*, and *AdWeek*. To learn more about Bruce, visit him at https://bruceturkel.com.

Why Do You Avoid Feedback?

The highest-paid people in the world love feedback. If you are Tiger Woods, Floyd Mayweather, Cristiano Rolando, Lionel Messi, LeBron

James, Roger Federer, Phil Mickelson, Manny Pacquiao, Kevin Durant, or Lewis Hamilton, you love feedback.

According to *Forbes*, the annual rankings of top earning athletes look at salaries, prize money, bonuses, endorsements, appearance fees, and licensing income. The Top 10 for the decade, which includes a pair from boxing, soccer, basketball, and golf, collectively made 6.1 billion U.S. dollars.

That is 10 people who love feedback. They made 6.1 billion U.S. dollars. Yes, you heard me right, billion with a B.

So, why do you avoid feedback? Feedback can be painful, and it shows us our shortcomings, our weaknesses, and areas of our game we need to improve. And, this is why, the 10 highest-paid athletes in the world have coaches and mentors. They have coaches and mentors that they pay to give them feedback.

To be their best, they have to work diligently on improving their weaknesses. Many times, the improvement only removes seconds or inches off their shot, stroke, or follow-through.

As Ken Blanchard says, "Feedback is the breakfast of champions."

I will ask this again, why are we afraid of feedback? We should not be. If we want to improve our skills and performance, it will require looking into the mirror of feedback. And many times, that is asking our managers, boss, or coworkers what they honestly think about an area we are trying to improve.

Do not allow fear of the truth to keep you from exposing your weaknesses or areas of improvement.

In the *Harvard Business Review* article "Fear of Feedback," Jay M. Jackman and Myra H. Strober say, "Those who learn to adapt to feedback can free themselves from old patterns. They can learn to acknowledge negative emotions, constructively reframe fear and criticism, develop realistic goals, create support systems, and reward themselves for achievements along the way."

The only thing to fear about feedback is nothing. Learn to embrace feedback; no, learn to run after it, and free yourself from the fear and worry about what others think. Who knows, you may become the highest-paid member on your team by facing your fear head-on!

As a Project Management Office (PMO) manager, director, or Chief information officer (CIO) of an organization, you are charged with facing your fears head-on and providing solutions that can help your organization become one of the top-performing firms in your industry. Are you avoiding feedback on how your project management organization is operating? In the same way that top athletes flourish by getting feedback from their coaches and mentors, the best-run organizations in the world flourish by understanding their PMO maturity levels and taking action on the feedback and insight they receive when completing a maturity assessment.

The purpose of a PMO 360 Maturity Assessment is to develop a roadmap of initiatives and actions that will enable your organization to achieve its vision, goals, and objectives and optimize its resource capabilities to deliver benefits and outcomes needed to accomplish your organization's mission.

Assessing your organization's capability in project portfolio management requires a systematic framework that you can use to define the nature of your organization's project management processes, an approach that is objective and allows comparisons both within and across industries is required. A PMO 360 Maturity Assessment allows you to define the present state of your organization's project, program, and portfolio management processes and address the gaps that will prevent you from achieving your target state for your organization.

To test drive a free copy of a PMO 360 Assessment, go to https://principlesofexecution.nsvey.net/ns/n/PMO360.aspx, and you will receive a customized report of your results!

"In a recent study of 51,896 executives, for example, those who ranked at the bottom 10% in asking for feedback (that is to say, they asked for feedback less often than fully 90% of their peers) were rated at the 15th percentile in overall leadership effectiveness. On the other hand, leaders who ranked at the top 10% in asking for feedback were rated, on average, at the 86th percentile in overall leadership effectiveness."

Jazz washes away the dust of everyday life.

—Art Blakey

When you begin to see the possibilities of music, you desire to do something really good for people, to help humanity free itself from its hangups. . . I want to speak to their souls.

—John Coltrane

Jazz Guitarist Chuck Loeb Loved Feedback

Chuck Loeb was not afraid of feedback. He picked up the guitar at a young age and discovered jazz at the age of 16. Chuck was born in Nyack, New York, and lived near New York City.

To develop his jazz guitar playing, he knew he would need direction, help, and feedback on what worked and what did not work. He listened to the jazz guitar playing of jazz greats like Wes Montgomery, George Benson, Zhu McLaughlin, and Pat Martino.

However, he knew that he would need hands-on instructions. So, he pursued and studied with jazz greats like Dennis Sandale and Jim Hall. After high school, he too spent two years in Boston at the Berkeley College of Music.

His professional career included playing jazz guitar with the group Steps Ahead with Michael Brecher and the band Fourplay, where he replaced Larry Carlton as their guitarist.

Chuck married a jazz singer named Carmen Cuesta, and they had a daughter, Lizzy, who also became a jazz singer. Chuck recorded an album with his wife and daughter and was nominated for a Grammy in 2015. Chuck passed away from cancer on July 31, 2017, but not before creating a legacy as a jazz guitar great.

A featured article on JazzTime.com stated: "The music scene has suffered a devastating blow," said bassist and longtime associate Will Lee in an email to JT. "Master guitarist and composer Chuck Loeb were so musical; he was one of those big-eared geniuses that heard the music in everyone and everything around him. Playing with Chuck on so many occasions, I can tell you that he had a way of utilizing my talents to get just what he needed out of me. He was so prolific—writing, producing and arranging for not only his projects but those of Carmen Cuesta, his multi-talented wife, daughters Lizzy Loeb and Christina Cuesta Loeb, as well as so many artists to whom he has contributed those talents. May Chuck's incredible spirit be remembered in his music for all time."

Chuck Loeb lived a full life as a jazz guitarist all because he was not afraid of seeking and running after feedback. The feedback that made him one of the most respected jazz guitarists of his time.

Jazz is a language that jazz musicians are consistently learning to speak better through their instruments. Jazz musicians are also consistently learning from each other as they perform and practice. Being open to feedback is critical for a jazz musician to grow and flourish. Here are a few additional benefits to being open to feedback.

Ten Benefits of Being Open to Feedback to Creating High-Performing Agile Project Teams

1. You will change and grow. One of the greatest benefits to feedback is when you see yourself changing from the input you have received and are acting upon. When you see a change in how you think and in your behavior because of the feedback you received and the input that you have gained from others, you grow in your confidence, and you understand that change for the better is possible.

2. Improves your listening skills. When we are open to feedback and where asking others for their input, we tend to listen to what they say much more carefully and attentively then if we had not asked for their feedback. This continuous exercise of intentionally listening or actively listening improves your listening ability in every area of your life.

3. Increases motivation. Seeing yourself change and improve increases your motivation for growth. Motivation is somewhat like a snowball rolling downhill. The more it stays in motion, the larger it gets, and the more motivation, the greater the speed gain.

4. Enhances your performance. When you are open to feedback, and you are implementing the advice and recommendations that you are receiving from your trusted colleagues, coaches, and mentors, you will begin to see your performance and skills improve. By enhancing your performance, you will create an upward spiral effect and an upward trajectory to high levels of accomplishment.

5. Continuous growth. As you experience continuous change, improved listening skills, increased motivation, and greater levels of performance, you will begin to grow. You will begin to grow personally and professionally. You will begin to crave and desire to grow because you would have tapped into the essence of being human. And, as human beings, we desire to grow and change to become all that we were created and put on this earth to become,

so by being open to feedback you are giving yourself the gift of continuous growth.

6. Increases your self-esteem and builds trust. You will also build trust, trust within yourself, and the trust of others. When you are reaching out to someone for feedback, and you put their recommendations into action and then follow up and let them know that you have put them into action, you will gain their respect, and they will develop a deeper level of trust. You are proving to be a man or woman of your word.

7. Develop closer relationships. Developing deeper levels of trust automatically leads to developing deeper and closer relationships on a personal and professional level. When the family and colleagues understand that they can rely on you and that you are a person of your word, you will lay the groundwork for deeper relationships.

8. Widens your horizon. As you continuously go after feedback, another benefit is that you are exposing yourself to others' points of views. You are opening your eyes; you see the world through someone else's perspective.

9. Improves your decision-making ability. You will improve your decision-making ability by making it a habit to seek the input and advice of others. This will widen your horizon and deepen your relationships. You are now on a path of continuous growth and building trust with yourself and those around you. And, as the good book says, "with many advisers, victory is sure."

10. Increases your possibility of thinking. Possibility thinking is the result of being continuously exposed to other points of view.

So, when you think about all of the benefits that we just covered, you can see that champions understand the value of seeking feedback. What about you?

Are you open to going after feedback? Here is how you can test your openness to feedback. Open your calendar and count the number of appointments you have had in the last month where you asked someone for input on how to improve in any area of your personal or professional life. How many appointments did you count?

The second way to tell how open you are to feedback is to look at your bank statement or checkbook. How much did you spend last month on coaching, mentoring, online training, or books or audio programs? How much did you spend looking for feedback to get better last month?

The benefits of feedback are like the benefits of lifting weights or practicing music. You only receive those benefits when you go to the gym and work out. Here is additional benefit feedback, so let us look at the neuroscience of feedback and how feedback impacts our brain.

The Neuroscience of Feedback

In his book *Social*, Dr. Matthew D. Lieberman discovered that our brains love positive feedback. He found that our brain responds to positive feedback as if it were the same as a physical reward. Dr. Lieberman writes, "Other studies have suggested that our brains crave the positive evaluation of others almost to an embarrassing degree. Keise Izuma conducted a study in Japan in which participants in the scanner saw that strangers had characterized them as sincere or dependable. Having someone we have never met and have no expectation of meeting provide us with tepid praise doesn't seem like it would be rewarding. And yet it reliably activated the subjects' reward systems. When participants in this study also completed a financial reward task, Izuma found that the social and financial rewards activated the same parts of the ventral striatum, a key component of the reward system to a similar degree."

Lieberman, Matthew D. *Social*. Crown, Kindle Edition, pp. 77–78.

When we provide each other with feedback and encouragement, our brain releases the neurochemicals oxytocin and dopamine. These chemicals provide us with a rush of positive emotions. We find ourselves more attracted to the group and see them as our tribe, people we want to be around and work with.

So, let us use the following agile skills to build up our teammates and get the positive juices flowing.

Six Agile Skills You Need to Master to Generate Positive Feedback on Your Team

1. Interpersonal skills
   Quadrants of emotional intelligence. Jeanne Segal, PhD, Melinda Smith, MA., Lawrence Robinson, and Jennifer Shub in their article

"Improving Emotional Intelligence (EQ)," published on helpguide. org, define emotional intelligence as "the ability to understand, use, and manage your own emotions in positive ways to relieve stress, communicate effectively, empathize with others, overcome challenges and defuse conflict. Emotional intelligence helps you build stronger relationships, succeed at school and work, and achieve your career and personal goals. It can also help you to connect with your feelings, turn intention into action, and make informed decisions about what matters most to you."

Someone with low emotional intelligence will want to be in control and is not open to receiving feedback. They are also not great at giving feedback. They tend to be confrontational and opinionated as well as not able to see things from someone else's point of view.

Psychologist Joseph Luft and Harry Ingham developed the foursquare Johari Window to help team members identify where they fall within the relationship among each other. The purpose of the window is to have a dialog with the team to determine how much you know about yourself and how much team members know about you. The goal is for each team member to move into the open quadrant in the upper left corner of the window.

The Johari Window

| Open: Known to self and others | Blind: Not known to self but known to others |
| Hidden: Known to self but not to others | Unknown: Not known to self or others |

2. Active listening

According to businessdictionary.com, active listening is defined as, "The act of mindfully hearing and attempting to comprehend the meaning of words spoken by another in a conversation or speech. Activity listening is an important business communication skill, and it can involve making sounds that indicate attentiveness, as well as the listener giving feedback in the form of a paraphrased rendition of what has been said by the other party for their confirmation."

Read more: http://businessdictionary.com/definition/active-listening.html

There are three levels of active listening:

- Internal listening. While in conversations with other team members, you tend to listen more to your internal dialog instead of focusing on what the other person is saying and how they are saying it.
- Focused listening. During focused listening, you are listening intently to others in the conversation and paying close attention to the details.
- Global listening. At this level, you are intentionally listening and can observe the emotional state of the person speaking.

3. Facilitation

According to the Agilealliance.org, an agile facilitator is "a person who chooses or is given the explicit role of conducting a meeting. This role usually entails that the facilitator will take little part in the discussions on the meeting's topic, but will focus primarily on creating the conditions for effective group processes, in the pursuit of the objectives for which the meeting was convened."

So, in other words, the agile facilitator is to play a non-biased role and help coordinate, organize, and support the project team and its various meetings. Four of the key objectives for the agile facilitator are too:

1. Set goals and objectives for the meeting.
2. Establish ground rules.
3. Chair the meeting and keep the meeting on time. They have the responsibility to start the meeting on time and end the meeting on time while making sure they have enough time to cover everything on the meeting's agenda.
4. And assist the project team as they see fit.

4. Negotiation

For a negotiation to be successful, the agile practitioner should embrace an attitude of win–win when negotiating with a team member, product owner, or project sponsor. Win–win negotiation is a mindset. It is a mindset of fairness and inclusivity. The goal of win–win is that everyone walks away from the negotiation feeling like they have been treated fairly and respectfully. The only other options to a win–win negotiation is win–lose, or lose–win.

Neither win–lose nor lose–win is the ideal situation. You and the person you are negotiating with will feel taken advantage of and manipulated. So, the only honest method of negotiation is to seek win–win.

5. Conflict resolution

- Level 1: Problem to solve. This is the level of everyday conflict, although there may be misunderstandings and miscommunication, the conversations are not emotionally charged. Team members are speaking in the present and are not making accusations to bring up unresolved conflicts from the past. Problems are being shared openly, and although it is uncomfortable, solutions are being reached.
- Level 2: Disagreement. In this level, conversations go from being specific to being general. Team members begin to distance themselves and are more focused on protecting their positions than on sharing all of the details of the issue and seeking a solution to the problem.
- Level 3: Contest. At this level, conversations have gone from win–win to win–lose or lose–win. Team members become historical and may also become hysterical, as they continually bring up issues from the past that have not been resolved. At this point, team members may also become cliquish and create alliances, causing further splintering of the team, and the problem becomes synonymous with the person.
- Level 4: Crusade. At this level, team members began to look for an out. Either they will leave the team or the person that they are considering to be the problem has to leave the team.
- Level 5: World war. At this level, team members are at war and are no longer interested, and the other person wins. They are bent on destroying each other, and the only answer is to separate the warring team members.

One of the best practices to prevent the team from reaching Levels 3, 4, or 5 is to intervene at the beginning of the project and establish team values and norms. Also, establishing rules of engagement collaboratively will help mitigate this volcano from erupting.

Convergence. The purpose of convergence is to collectively get everyone on the same page and agree on the best answer. This will create buy-in, as everyone on the team has had the opportunity to share their opinion and obtain clarification.

Shared collaboration. The purpose of the shared collaboration is for the team to reach a consensus on an approach or with a critical decision.

6. Participatory Decision-Making

The participatory decision-making process provides a vehicle to fairly make a decision when a consensus agreement cannot be reached. This approach combines the principles of convergence and shared collaboration to reach an agreement the agile team can live with.

- Simple voting. This is a simple voting process of asking each team member if they are for or against the decision. The majority wins.
- Thumbs up or down or sideways. This approach is similar to being voted on in the Roman Coliseum, except for the sideways thumb. The sideways thumb is the symbol for *I cannot decide*. Again, the majority wins unless the sideways thumbs are in the majority.
- Fist of five. This approach allows team members to display to what degree they approve or reject the decision based on the number of figures they display. The scoring range goes from one figure (I agree) to holding up five figures (I disagree).

Discover High-Performing Team Feedback Tool

Following is a list of applications and online tools you can use to help facilitate your feedback process.

Top 360 Degree Feedback Software https://getapp.com/p/sem/360-degree-feedback-software

Assessment Questions

1. What have you learned in this chapter that can help you and your team provide better feedback with one another?

   _____

   _____

   _____

2. How will you and your team go about using the insight about being open to the feedback you have learned in this chapter?

   _____

   _____

   _____

3. What steps will you take to implement a more positive feedback strategy on your current and future projects?

   _____

   _____

   _____

4. What do Bruce's and Chuck's stories have in common that helped them to manage feedback as they pursued their dreams and goals through their life's ups and downs?

   _____

   _____

   _____

5. How can you use the agile feedback skills we discussed to increase the positive emotions on your team?

   _____

   _____

   _____

Additional Resources

- The Johari Window: Helping Build Trust Through Communication: https://educational-business-articles.com/johari-window/
- Coaching agile teams to constructively navigate conflict: https://pmi.org/learning/library/coaching-agile-project-teams-navigate-conflict-6760
- Fear of feedback: https://hbr.org/2003/04/fear-of-feedback

CHAPTER 7

Visualize Your Results

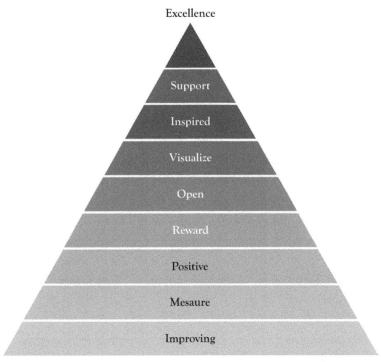

Excellence

Support

Inspired

Visualize

Open

Reward

Positive

Mesaure

Improving

Workplace Jazz Framework

Imagination is more important than knowledge. For a while, knowledge defines all we currently know and understand, imagination points to all we might yet discover and create.

—Albert Einstein

All successful men and women are big dreamers. They imagine what their future could be, ideal in every respect, and then they work every day toward their distant vision, that goal or purpose.

—Brian Tracy

It takes a dream to get started, desires to keep going, and determination to finish.

—Eddie Harris

This chapter will teach you the value of visualizing your goals and the impact it can have on you in the same way it influences world-class musicians and athletes. They have learned the secret of visualizing their goals and outcomes, and after reading this chapter, so will you.

Next, you will read a story about a friend of mine and a schoolteacher who started a children's choir at the Strathmore concert hall, which has become one of the top children's choirs in the country, and how he visualized the results he wanted for his program.

Next, we will discuss the high-performance secrets from Kirk Whalum, a Grammy-winning saxophonist who has recorded over 20 albums during his prolific career, and how on his last project, Humanite, he traveled the world recording with up-and-coming artists from every continent.

We will also dive into the world of neuroscience and look at what that science says about the power of visualization and how it affects our brain.

We will finish this chapter discussing how you can adopt these visualization concepts and techniques and build a high-performing agile team, and we will look at some of the tools that are available to you as an agile practitioner.

The Strathmore Children's Chorus found its purpose by having the vision to serve.

—Chris Guerra

The Strathmore Children's Chorus began in 2012, and at its inception, we knew we needed to establish a culture of servanthood and customer service with our staff. Everyone needed to understand the importance of culture and how it will play out in our organization.

The vision and motivation for starting the children's chorus were to offer a musical experience in the community that was unique and attached to one of the strongest musical organizations in the Washington, DC, area, which was the Strathmore Music Center. It was rather apparent that no children's chorus was available in our local community that offered a high-quality choral organization at a reasonable price and would allow the children to experience a professional singing opportunity.

The community around Montgomery County, Maryland, and beyond previously had only one children's chorus that was a 99 percent homogeneous cultured ensemble, which wasn't reaching most of the children that made up our diverse community. We wanted an organization that would be reflective of the diverse makeup of Montgomery County and beyond.

So, it all started with a vision I had after I researched and collected information on the children's chorus in our area. Also, I gathered my findings into a business case that I pitched to the president and CEO of Strathmore, and they were very excited about it and had actually wanted to start a children's chorus upon its inception, but other programs had to come first.

In the first year, we had six members come out for our very first audition. After that, the floodgates opened, and we finished up the first year with over 100 students in the program. We had only anticipated about 20 to 30 children would join. The research had shown that a new children's chorus normally would start its first year with about 20 members. After the first year, the quality of the ensemble grew, and the number of children wanting to participate kept growing, and we ended up with over 200 students by the end of the year. We became the fastest growing children's chorus in the United States in our second year. We decided to cap the membership to around 225 children with a breakdown of five different choral groups.

What I learned in the process of developing the Strathmore Children's Chorus is that there has to be a strong visionary leader to take any organization forward and to pass their vision along to the other staff members and the children and parents. We wanted to be a high-quality group and participate with other professional organizations within the Washington, DC, area. We also wanted to put ourselves on a national level as a world-class musical organization. We have been meeting a number of our goals by performing with the National Philharmonic and with the National Philharmonic Chorale group twice, and we've opened for Tony Bennett and Julie Andrews. It has been wonderful to have these unique opportunities for our singers and our staff members as well.

I believe that the greatest thing a leader should do is to craft a vision; I see it as the number one role of a leader. You can look at the book *The Leadership Challenge* by Kouzes and Posner, where you will also see that developing a vision is the number one role of the leader. Any organization that is going to excel has to have a leader with a compelling vision, and that will draw its members in and its clients as well. Then they need to stay true to their vision.

I believe that developing a culture of success was pivotal to the achievements and goals of the Strathmore Children's Chorus in our first few years. Each staff member had to know we were educators with music as our vehicle and customer service as our mantra. We were there to serve. We supported the parents as parents and educated our young artists through the discipline of choral music.

The Strathmore Music Center is known throughout the DC area for extraordinary excellence in all and any production it undertakes. Excellence is one of our core values, and customer service is our mantra. To develop this culture of service to build our brand and our singers, it had to flow steadily through every staff meeting, rehearsal, and performance. Each child was treated like a star.

Christopher G. Guerra is the founder and artistic director emeritus of the Strathmore Children's Chorus, located in North Bethesda, Maryland, with performances at the Strathmore Music Center. Strathmore is one of the fastest-growing children's choruses in the United States, with over 225 singers and five ensembles in its first two years.

Statistical Proof that Visualizing Your Goals Work!

According to an article on Forbes.com titled "Survey Shows Visualizing Success Works," by Eilene Zimmerman:

"TD Bank surveyed over 1,100 entrepreneurs and 500 small business owners to understand how visualizing their goals affected their outcomes. 76% of those business owners said that today their business is where they envisioned it would be when they started it. Many used vision boards and visualization practices to enhance their experience.

TD Bank partnered with the psychologist Barbara Nussbaum, who specializes in the emotional and psychological implications of money, to analyze its survey results. Nussbaum says 'by visualizing our personal and related financial goals, we can focus on them more, they feel more real, and they feel more possible. We also become better at actually moving toward them, she says. Why? With a vision board, which usually has images, photos, sometimes objects (a piece of fabric, a dried flower, etc.) and words, Nussbaum says we are immersing ourselves in our goals, in a multi-sensory, experiential way—through words, ideas, vision, and feeling.'

Do you spend time visualizing your personal or team goals? How much further along would you be if you practice visualization daily?

If you want to reach a goal, you must "see the reaching" in your own mind before you arrive at your goal.

—Zig Ziglar

High-Performance Secrets of Kirk Whalum: Visualize What You Want

Growing up in Memphis, Tennessee, Kirk learned to play "Amazing Grace" at his father's church. Little did he know that "Amazing Grace" would be the song Whitney Houston would ask him to solo on in front of a mixed crowd in a concert in South Africa after the fall of apartheid.

After attending Texas Southern University, he came on the jazz scene, working as a sideman before stepping out as a melodic saxophonist leading his bands. He has performed with Bob James, Luther Vandross, Quincy Jones, and Whitney Houston, to name a few.

His musical philosophy is to put yourself in the music and dare to be you. In keeping true to his vision, he released an album in 2017 called *Love Covers*. #Lovecovers is also the hashtag that Kirk Whalum used for the project. His vision for the record was the idea that God's love covers us all. #Lovecover is not only the name of this hit album, but it has become a movement.

His most recent album, *Humanite*, promotes the vision of valuing each other, loving our fellow man and woman.

After recording multiple albums, Kurt had a vision of reaching out and lifting up young artists from around the world. Kirk performed on several world tours; these tours opened his eyes to the immense talent that is available on every continent. Kirk discovered that these talented musicians were not receiving the airtime and visibility that other musicians received. So, his goal was to record an album called "Humanite" to highlight up-and-coming artists from around the world. This album would highlight these talented musicians along with other local artists from their countries with the mindset of exposing the world to these up-and-coming artists. Kurt reached his goal, and the album *Humanite* was released in 2019.

The power of visualizing is to develop the essence of who you are and who you want to become. Not an imitation of someone else, but an authentic future version of yourself.

To learn more about Kirk Whalum, go to https://kirkwhalum.com/.

Jazz musicians become jazz musicians by learning from other experts. No one is born a jazz musician; it is a learned skill. But first, the musician must experience it by seeing an expert who has developed their skills at a higher level.

Top 10 Ways that Visualizing Improves Your Results

1. Visualizing activates your reticular activating system (RAS). The RAS is like a filter for the brain. Once you identify a goal or focus on an object, the RAS becomes a heat-seeking missile that finds every instance of that item within your environment. For example, after you purchased your last car, did you not see everyone else who had the same car and the same color, which you did not notice before? That is your RAS in operation. So, the purpose is to visualize our goals in such a way that engages our RAS to identify all the detailed components and elements that we will need to achieve that goal.

2. It builds motivation. Visualizing increases your motivation because as you begin to see the steps to accomplishing your goals, as they become clearer, you will be more excited and motivated to accomplish them. And, as you begin to accomplish the small steps leading to the larger goal, it will create this snowball motivational effect.

3. It provides clarity for your mission, vision, and goals. Because of the RAS and now the new motivation that you have to accomplish your goals, you also begin to see your overall mission and vision for your goals. This is especially true if you spend time daily visualizing the outcomes of achieving your goal and also writing out your goals as affirmations.

4. It enhances possibility thinking. Possibility thinking is enhanced because as you see the completion of action steps toward your goals, you will know that achieving your goal is possible.

5. It improves your recognition of resources. Visualizing your goals and outcomes again activates the RAS, which is the filter by which we see the world that we live in. By activating the RAS toward your specific goals, you will begin to notice resources that are within your reach that you had not seen before because they were being filtered out of your view. You begin to recognize resources such as books that provide information toward achieving your goal. People within your network, and even the financial resources needed to accomplish your goal, will become visible.

6. It improves coordination and concentration. If your goal requires you to become better at a physical activity, you will notice that you will begin to improve dramatically in this area. This will happen because our brains do not know the difference between visualizing an outcome and living an outcome. So, by practicing through visualization, you will begin to strengthen your neural network, which is responsible for coordination and concentration around that physical activity.

7. It enhances your motor skills. The reason that most world-class musicians and athletes use visualization as a part of their regular practice is because it refines their motor skills for the task at hand. I stated earlier your brain does not know the difference between mentally practicing through visualization or practicing through physically performing the activity. Your neural network will be activated and strengthen each time you mentally practice and visualize yourself completing the activity.

8. It improves your brain wiring. Visualization strengthens your brain's wiring. Just like walking through a field creates a path, visualizing an activity strengthens the neural network and creates a path where signals in the brain can travel faster with more efficiency and a stronger signal.

9. It improves your ability to learn faster. By practicing visualization, which strengthens the wiring in our brain, it facilitates our ability to learn information faster than practicing the material without visualization.

10. It improves your decision-making skills. Because visualization strengthens our brain's ability to learn information faster and has a better awareness of the information and activates the RAS, it also enhances our ability to make better decisions faster because now we have crystallized the information that we need to make better decisions.

The Agile Mindset

The following charts and graphs are great tools for visualizing your team's performance. As an agile practitioner, these charts will help you to see your current and future work, backlog items, and forecast future activities.

Tracking Team Performance

• Burndown charts with story points. Display how quickly the team is working on completing a user story and customer requirements.

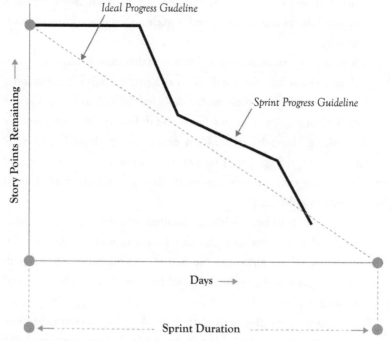

Figure 7.1 Burndown chart for an active sprint

- Burn-up charts. Display how many user story points are in the backlog compared to how many the team has completed.

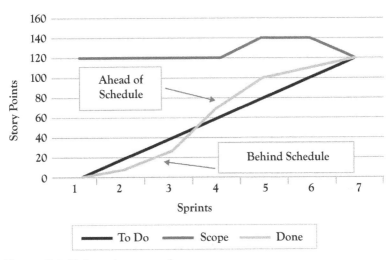

Figure 7.2 Release burn-up chart

- Velocity. Displays how much value is delivered during each sprint. How much was planned compared to how much is being delivered?

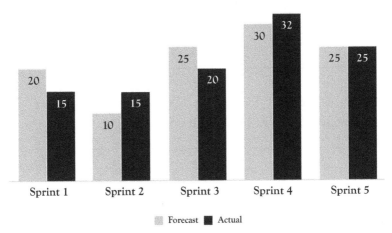

Figure 7.3 Velocity

- Cumulative flow. Displays an area chart that shows the project work in progress for a specific period.

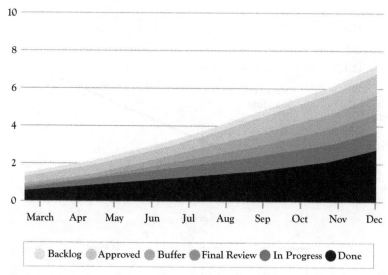

Figure 7.4 Cumulative flow diagram

Assessment Questions

1. What have you learned in this chapter that can help you and your team visualize your results and outcomes better?

———————————————————————————

———————————————————————————

———————————————————————————

2. How will you and your team go about using the insight about visualization that you have learned in this chapter?

———————————————————————————

———————————————————————————

———————————————————————————

3. What steps will you take to implement visualization on your current and future projects?

_____

_____

_____

4. What do Chris's and Kirk's stories have in common that helped them visualize their results as they pursued their dreams and goals?

_____

_____

_____

5. How can you use the agile charts and graphs we discussed to improve the results you are getting with your team and on your projects?

_____

_____

_____

Additional Resources

- Visualization Techniques to Affirm Your Desired Outcomes: A Step-by-Step Guide https://wjackcanfield.com/blog/visualize-and-affirm-your-desired-outcomes-a-step-by-step-guide/
- 11 Tips For Visualizing Something You Want & Actually Making It Happen https://bustle.com/p/11-tips-for-visualizing-something-you-want-actually-making-it-happen-2334759
- THE IMPORTANCE OF VISUALIZING YOUR GOALS https://unfinishedsuccess.com/the-importance-of-visualizing-your-goals/
- Seeing Is Believing: The Power of Visualization https://psychologytoday.com/us/blog/flourish/200912/seeing-is-believing-the-power-visualization

CHAPTER 8

Inspired by Aspirations

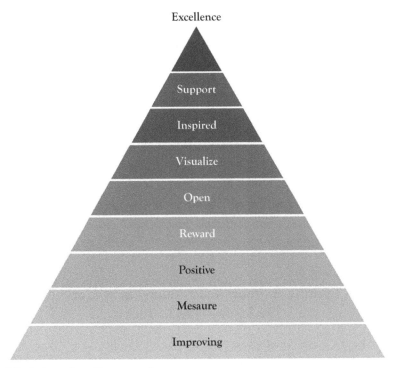

Workplace Jazz Framework

The history of jazz lets us know that this period in our history is not the only period we've come through together. If we truly understood the history of our national arts, we'd know that we have mutual aspirations, a shared history, in good times, and bad.

—Wynton Marsalis

It is not for man to rest in absolute contentment. He is born to hopes and aspirations as the sparks fly upward unless he has brutified his nature and quenched the spirit of immortality, which is his portion.

—Southey

This chapter will teach you how to analyze and distinguish between being inspired to accomplish a goal and having aspirational goals and dreams. There is a neurological difference. Learn how musicians inspire each other in the moment for a more heartfelt performance.

Jim Cathcart, a passionate guitar player and Hall of Fame speaker, shares how he helped Harley Davidson ignite their team to aspirational leadership.

Next, we will discuss how developing high-performing agile teams is aspirational and requires establishing a long-term vision of the organization becoming agile.

We will also look into the power of aspirations and its effect on your team's collaboration.

You will meet Freddie Ravel, a number-one hit recording artist who transformed himself into a world-class keynote artist who helps individuals and organizations aspire to greatness by teaching and illustrating the power of melody, harmony, and rhythm.

We will finish this chapter looking at the neuroscience of aspirations, its benefits, and how you can implement an aspiration mindset in your agile teams.

Igniting Aspirational Leadership at Harley Davidson—Jim Cathcart

I've been a professional speaker and author for 40-plus years. I've worked with 3,000 organizations around the world, and I've come to notice what makes for a harmonious organization and what needs to be in a place where there's a lot of discord. When Walt Disney wanted to build Disneyland and built the original promotion to draw people there, he found that his job had changed and he was no longer the builder and marketer. He needed to be the guy who was keeping the flame, the one who kept the spirit of Disneyland alive. He got everyone who worked there to realize they were a cast member, and not just an employee, and to treat everyone as a guest.

Likewise, Isadore Sharp, as the founder and creator of the Four Seasons Hotel chain worldwide, found that as his company evolved, his role changed similarly. And what he does today is he flies around the world to his various properties and inspires and reminds the staff of the role they had in serving the top level of travelers in a very elegant way. If you look at a rowing team, just reach from example to example here, a rowing team, with all the strength and all the talk in the world, would be ineffective if some of the rowers were not in sync with the other rowers. So, there's got to be someone kind of calling the beat and saying "stroke, stroke, stroke" so that everyone can match that pace and rhythm and get the maximum force from each person's ability or strength applied to that rowing. Likewise, in an orchestra, the same thing is true, or a band. It is the bass and the drums that keep the beat, and that gives the background feel. But that's not what inspires people. That's not what engages people at first. What inspires them is the conductor, or lyricist, or the person that's putting their emotion into the performance, and the sharing with everybody who's participating gets it. What all of this is about. I once did a speaking engagement for Harley-Davidson, and they said we want to hear you speak before we hire you. I said no, you want to see if I get it who Harley-Davidson is. They said good point. How do we find that out? I said, put a motorcycle under me, and let's ride. I ended up being their speaker, and it went really, really well, and I had a great motorcycle ride.

You see, an organization is just a lengthened shelter of the individuals who inspired it in the first place. To keep that shelter big enough, to provide shade for everyone and inspiring enough that I want to be a part of it, the leader has to remain the catalyst and cheerleader for aspirational change and inspire people to remember the vision.

Jim Cathcart, CSP, CPAE, is the founder and CEO of Cathcart. com. A Sales and Marketing Hall of Fame inductee, he is the author of *Relationship Selling* and *The Self-Motivation Handbook*.

Merriam-Webster defines aspiration as: "A strong desire to achieve something high or great. . . for example, an aspiration to become an expert."

https://merriam-webster.com/dictionary/aspiration

Developing a high-performing agile team is aspirational and requires establishing a long-term vision of the organization becoming agile.

According to the article on how to mess up your agile transformation in seven easy missteps, McKinsey consulting firm states that Misstep 1 is "Not having alignment on the aspiration and value of an agile transformation."

https://mckinsey.com/business-functions/organization/our-insights/
how-to-mess-up-your-agile-transformation-in-seven-easy-missteps

---

*Aspirational leaders spend more time building their team and delegating,
which helps their team members to grow.*

The Power of Aspirations

*We aspire by doing things, and the things we do change us so that we
can do the same things, or things of that kind, better and better.*

*The work of aspiration includes, but is by no means limited to, the
mental work of thinking, imagining, and reasoning. If a callow youth
gets an inkling of the value of classical music or painting or wine and
wants to come to appreciate these values more fully, it will not suffice
for him to think carefully about these things. He must listen to music
or visit museums or drink wine.*

—Callard, Agnes. *Aspiration*. Oxford University Press,
Kindle Edition, 2018

*Positional leaders ignore the fact that every person has hopes, dreams,
desires, and goals of his own. And leaders must bring their vision and the
aspirations of the people they lead together in a way that benefits everyone.*

—John C. Maxwell

High-Performance Secrets from Freddie Ravel

Freddie Ravel grew up in Los Angeles and began his musical training at
an early age. After high school, he attended California State University,
where he studied music and received a bachelor's degree. According to a
Smooth Views Magazine interview with Shannon West, "He released Sol
to Soul a few years later, then in 2001, his self-titled GRP release delivered

the #1 hit, 'Sunny Side Up.' He joined Sergio Mendes' band when he was 23 and has collaborated with an array of musical stars . . . including Herbie Hancock, Madonna, Jennifer Lopez, and Prince. He was also the musical director for Earth, Wind, and Fire and later for Al Jarreau."

It was three months later, after receiving the news of his number-one hit, that the world experienced 9/11. Shortly afterward, during a concert with Al Jarreau in South Africa, the country was plagued with people dying from AIDS, and when Freddie returned home, his wife informed him that she was pregnant. It was during this time that Freddie began to question his aspirations and musical journey.

Although Freddie knew he would always be a recording artist and a performing musician, he felt a calling to do something more with his life and to have a greater impact on humanity. His aspiration changed from being a performing and recording artist to becoming someone who used music to teach individuals and organizations the principles he had learned performing with many of the greatest performing artists of our time.

To address this new aspiration, Freddie developed a presentation entitled "Tune UP to Success," in which he focuses on the musical elements of melody, harmony, and rhythm. These are all elements of music that he translates into activities we perform in business, and he uses his music performance to illustrate the dynamics of listening, leading, and collaborating all wrapped around a cadence of execution through time management. During the interview, Freddie shared, "A CNN poll showed that 83 percent of Americans don't like what they do for a living and there's a Gallup poll showing that says 26 percent of Americans feel engaged in what they do. So that's 74 percent that don't."

Freddie has gone on to share his message with organizations such as Del Monte, Coca Cola, and Walmart, to name only a few of the companies and organizations to whom he has delivered his performance of "Tune UP to Success."

To learn more about Freddie Ravel, visit his website at https://lifeintune.com/

Being a jazz musician is not about doing jazz; one has to aspire to be a jazz musician and embrace and embody the philosophy of jazz as a mindset.

The Neuroscience of Aspirations

Our brains are designed for growth, and when we have an aspirational focus, our brains are primed to embrace new knowledge and grow our neural network. This can be accomplished at any age or any point in our career, and it is all based on neuroplasticity.

It is open to influence and being curious. This engages the prefrontal cortex. According to the Coal Springs Harbor Laboratory DNA Learning Center, "The prefrontal cortex is thought to play an important role in higher brain functions. It is a critical part of the executive system, which refers to planning reasoning and judgment. It is also involved in personality and emotions by contributing to the assessment and control of appropriate social behaviors."

Neuroscientists have confirmed that having aspirations enlarges and increases our brain mass. So, what are the benefits of aspirations?

Benefits of Setting Aspirations

1. Aspirational teams help each other's brains release positive neurotransmitters, which help facilitate team bonding.
2. Aspirational thinking creates more mental space for the team to navigate. According to Judith E. Glaser in her book *Conversational Intelligence*, when we focus on understanding the needs and aspirations of others, we create a safe space for people to feel they belong on the same team. We bring the person whose stance is *wait and see* on board.
3. Aspirational teams have a higher level of trust. "According to sociologists Niklas Luhmann and John Coleman, trust is a risky decision whereby the trusting person risks being exploited, yet hopes that his or her trust will be rewarded by trustworthy behavior (Luhmann, 1968; Coleman, 1990). Also, trust increases the efficiency of social interaction. If people trust and trust is rewarded, everyone is typically better off compared with a situation in which no one trusts, and people act in an untrustworthy manner. Economist Kenneth Arrow, therefore, described trust as 'an important lubricant of a social system'" (Arrow, 1974).

4. Aspirational leaders spend more time building their team and delegating, which helps their team members to grow.

5. Aspirational teams are more in sync and in tune with each other's intentions.

The Agile Mindset

According to Judith E. Glaser in her book *Conversational Intelligence*, "You can shift the outcome of a meeting by starting with a trust-building activity. This signals the amygdala to slow down and be quiet, and allows other parts of the brain to actively seek data that says this will be a good, trusting experience. The best way to set up a meeting for increased trust is to start by establishing rules of engagement."

Develop Rules of Engagement at the Beginning of Projects and Important Meetings

1. Use a whiteboard or flipchart to capture the rules of engagement and write the words *Rules of Engagement* at the top of the page.

2. Inquire of everyone in the group to provide the actions or behaviors that will produce the best outcomes for the meeting. If meetings are normally dominated by one or two people in the group, have everyone write down their ideas on a Post-it note, and once they are done writing down their ideas, each person gets up and sticks their notes on the flip chart.

3. Then, group the words that are similar and create an affinity diagram of the terms that have been provided by the team. When the team uses terms like love or respect, then ask them to explain what they mean by using those terms. This will help everyone get on the same page as far as what each term means for the group.

4. Finally, capture from the group how feedback will be handled when someone violates the rules of engagement that everyone has agreed to. Also, clarify the process to resolve conflicts and escalation procedures when team members cannot agree on a principle that has been violated.

Assessment Questions

1. What have you learned in this chapter that can help you and your team become more aspirational with one another?

   _____

   _____

   _____

2. How will you and your team go about using the insight about being inspired to be aspirational with what you have learned in this chapter?

   _____

   _____

   _____

3. What steps will you take to implement to be more positive and aspirational on your current and future projects?

   _____

   _____

   _____

4. What do Jim's and Kirk's stories have in common that helped them to manage their aspirations as they pursued their dreams and goals?

   _____

   _____

   _____

5. How can you use the neuroscience of aspiration finding we discussed to increase a more positive outcome on your team?

   _____

   _____

   _____

Additional Resources

- The Power of Writing Down Your Goals and Dreams: https://huffpost.com/entry/the-power-of-writing-down_b_12002348
- What Are Your Aspirations? https://thindifference.com/2015/08/what-are-your-aspirations/
- Structuring your organization to meet global aspirations: https://mckinsey.com/~/media/mckinsey/dotcom/client_service/Organization/PDFs/Structuring_your_organization_to_meet_global_aspirations.ashx

CHAPTER 9

Surrender to Support

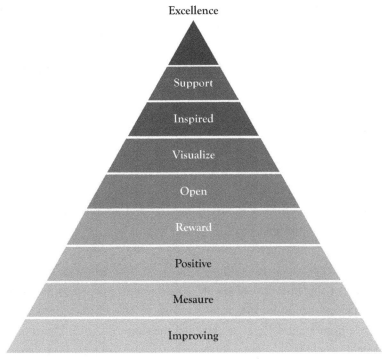

Excellence

Support

Inspired

Visualize

Open

Reward

Positive

Mesaure

Improving

Workplace Jazz Framework

Jazz does not belong to one race or culture but is a gift that America has given the world.

—Ahmad Alaadeen

This chapter will help you understand why jazz musicians willingly adapt to their consistently changing roles as one person solos and leads and everyone else surrenders and supports the soloist. And, how these skills are critical in today's ever-changing business environment.

Gaining Buy-In and Support in the Musical Upside Down

Sherwin Mackintosh is a dear friend, a musician/composer, who has spent over 40 years of his life making music in New York City and around the world.

On the topic of *buy-in from a culture perspective*, Sherwin told me:

One of the biggest challenges that I have seen for me was in the recent mounting of a musical, *Upside Down*, that I had written with my creative partner, Steve Johnson.

Upside Down was created in 1986 and had been performed in New York, Boston, and around the U.S. It was captured on video and had been viewed around the world. It was also translated into Russian and performed in Moscow and Kiev. So, the musical had a very devoted following worldwide, but this would be a new product and would require a lot of people to take three weeks out of their busy schedules and share our vision. We wanted to get the best people that we could, so we launched a nationwide search for actors, singers, dancers, and technicians who shared our passion for this musical.

Be a Part of History

As soon as we started asking people, their comment was, "I want to be part of this historical moment." These weren't our words, but soon became our mantra for the group. This would be a historic gathering of people from around the country to tell the story of Upside Down once again. It would be live-streamed around the world and recorded for a new generation. No one wanted to miss this opportunity.

Make It a Priority

We had amazing people in Broadway shows, the Metropolitan Opera, and TV who were interested. With their already busy lives, we had to get everyone to buy into the idea that this was going to be their next project; Upside Down was their next commitment. There would be sacrifices to be made, but everyone had to agree to make this a priority.

Share the Dream

Since so many people had seen the musical or were familiar with its songs and themes, it was not hard to sell people on our vision. These were people who shared our love for Upside Down and wanted to be part of this retelling. The vision was clear, attractive, and attainable.

Ride the Wave

As soon as people started making commitments to the project, there were inevitably obstacles that appeared. Schedules, other projects, family issues, and financial concerns tried to cloud the process, but we kept pointing people back to history, the priority, and the dream. We were able to ride the storm and to see the products sell out in a few weeks.

With total buy-in from everyone, the energy from the cast and crew at our first gathering was electric! The synergy from these stellar individual performers produced overwhelming, real emotions, and that translated into an incredible show. *Upside Down* was a huge success—a unified group with a common purpose and a total buy-in.

> *People buy into the leader before they buy into the vision.*
> —John C. Maxwell

> *Deep and sustainable change ... requires changes in behavior among those who do not welcome the change.*
> —Douglas B. Reeves, *Leading Change in Your School: How to Conquer Myths, Build Commitment, and Get Results*

Jazz musicians are consistently changing roles as one person solos and leads and everyone else surrenders and supports the soloist. This creates a beautiful musical conversation between the musicians.

According to the Gallup-Healthways Well-Being Index, some 52 percent of the U.S. workforce characterized themselves as not engaged during the first half of 2012. An additional 18 percent were actively disengaged. Gallup estimates the cost of this divide at 300 billion U.S. dollars annually.

Donald T. Phillips, in the book *Lincoln on Leadership*, says, "Lincoln understood the motives of men and how they tended to react under stress. As a result, he was very lenient of what was perceived by many to be cowardly conduct. The plain fact that Lincoln granted so many pardons just naturally helped him build successful affiliations with his followers.

Not that he granted pardons as a strategy for alliance-building. It was done rather because Lincoln was a kind and caring human being. But people are much more likely to trust a leader if they know he is compassionate and forgiving of mistakes. And trust, of course, is the essential building block for successful relationships."

A key to creating buy-in and support is to understand human nature. The leader should start with themselves first and then learn the personality of their teammates and followers.

The leader has to take time out of their busy schedule and spend time listening and connecting with their people.

Learn to generate hope within your people by including them in the process and co-creating your organization's strategy, goals, and objectives. People buy-in to and support what they help create.

No one wins a Super Bowl, a Stanley Cup, or an NBA championship or delivers a world-class symphony performance as an individual. It is always done as a team, where everyone is connected and working closely together. It is like their heartbeats have become synchronized as one. If someone has a great talent on the team, everyone else supports them because they are going to help the team achieve their goals. Think Tom Brady and the New England Patriots winning six Super Bowls.

According to Judith E. Glaser, in her book *Conversational Intelligence*, "Sometimes we unintentionally anger someone, or we say the wrong thing, or we get into a conflict without meaning to. This may happen at work, with customers, with friends, or within our own family. Conversational rituals can become part of everyday life to support people in bridging, connecting, and strengthening their relationships."

I believe we can take this even further, by making this philosophy, to be surrendered to support, a way of life. That is exactly what David Dyson, a jazz bassist, has done all of his career.

High-Performance Secrets from David Dyson

To understand the essence of this chapter on surrender to support, I would like for you to take a moment and click and go to the YouTube video entitled "DC BASSIST DAVID DYSON INTERVIEW w/PIECES OF A DREAM": https://youtu.be/VPcc_or7zMs.

As you watch the initial seven minutes of this video, I would like for you to pay attention to David Dyson, the bass player for Pieces of a Dream. Throughout his performance, David plays the supporting role, although he is one of the main composers and is the music director for Pieces of a Dream. During this performance, his entire role is to lay the foundation for the song and to provide a platform for the guitar player and the piano player to shine and solo; this is the essence of this chapter on being surrendered to support.

David was born in Rapid City, South Dakota, in 1965. His family moved to the Washington, DC, metro area when he was two years old. At the age of 12, David began playing bass guitar after being inspired by recordings of Larry Graham and Lewis Johnson from the group the Brothers Johnson.

David developed his skills as a bass player to the point that at the age of 14, his weekend job was laying down bass tracks in a studio in Clinton, Maryland, where he was paid 50 U.S. dollars a session. Not a bad gig for a teenager.

After high school, David moved to Boston, where he attended the Berklee College of Music, and after graduation, he secured a professional gig playing bass for Walter Beasley. According to Wikipedia and the interview clip I previously referenced, "In the fall of 1988 producer, Maurice Starr was searching for musicians for New Kids on the Block. Dyson auditioned and landed the gig as their bass player. He toured with them from 1989–1992 as their bassist and musical director."

Because David has embraced the philosophy of being surrendered to support, he has performed with headline jazz artists such as:

- Gerald Albright
- Philip Bailey
- Walter Beasley
- Rich Braun
- Dennis Chambers
- Candy Dulfer
- Debbie Gibson
- Wynton Marsalis
- Najee
- Maysa

- Jonathan Butler
- Peter White
- And many more

What is most interesting about David is his attitude regarding other bass players that he could look at as competitors. He views them as collaborators and colleagues. In many of his interviews, he consistently expresses his admiration and appreciation for their talent and skills, as well as their contribution to the art of playing bass. David Dyson has become one of the most in-demand bassists on the jazz scene today. Because of his ability to lay down bass tracks that other jazz musicians love to play over, he is the epitome of the surrender to support philosophy.

To learn more about David Dyson, go to http://daviddysonbass.com/

Jazz musicians are consistently changing roles as one person solos and leads and everyone else surrenders and supports the soloist. This creates a beautiful musical conversation between the musicians. They naturally understand that to make the music breathe, they will sometimes lead but will most often support the other musicians in the group.

It's the group sound that's important, even when you're playing a solo. You not only have to know your instrument; you must know the others and how to back them up at all times. That's jazz!

—Oscar Peterson

Principle of Surrender to Support—Defined

"The action of yielding one's person or giving up the possession of something especially into the power of another"

"To give (oneself) over to something (such as an influence)"

https://merriam-webster.com/dictionary/surrender

The Neuroscience of Support

According to the *Psychology Today* article, "The Neuroscience of Giving: Proof that helping others helps you," by Eva Ritvo MD:

Neuroscience has demonstrated that giving is a powerful pathway for creating more personal joy and improving overall health.

While the brain is remarkably complex, the neurochemical drivers of happiness are quite easy to identify. Dopamine, serotonin, and oxytocin make up the Happiness Trifecta. Any activity that increases the production of these neurochemicals will cause a boost in mood. It's that simple.

But the benefits don't stop at moods! Serotonin is connected to sleep, digestion, memory, learning, and appetite. Dopamine is connected to motivation and arousal. Oxytocin, "the cuddle hormone," is among the most ancient of our neurochemicals and has a powerful effect on the brain and the body. When oxytocin begins to flow, blood pressure decreases, and the foundation for sexual arousal is built. Bonding increases, social fears are reduced, and trust and empathy are enhanced. Oxytocin is also an anti-inflammatory and reduces pain and enhances wound healing. https://psychologytoday.com/us/blog/vitality/201404/the-neuroscience-giving

Are you convinced now about the benefits that being surrendered to support can have on your team and on yourself? It is the neuroscience of working together.

According to the *HBR* article "5 Ways to Help Your Team Be Open to Change" by Edith Onderick-Harvey, "For change to be operationalized, you need to inspire your team to be creative and enable them to innovate. But innovation only happens when people can work in the gray space—where ambiguity is okay and business principles, rather than hard and fast rules, apply."

The article also shares five things you can do to help your team embrace change and surrender to supporting the mission and each other. The five practices are:

1. Tell stories about others who moved beyond the status quo.
2. Create dialogue, inviting others to ask questions, and share emotions, experiences, and insights.
3. Ask *What if* questions in one-on-one and team meetings.
4. Set expectations that everyone (including yourself) should acknowledge and take responsibility for mistakes. And then, treat mistakes as opportunities for learning and growth.
5. Champion cross-boundary collaboration and networks to open up thinking and gain new perspectives. https://hbr.org/2019/04/5-ways-to-help-your-team-be-open-to-change

How Can You Make Surrendering to Support Your Philosophy?

1. Think and focus on others more than yourself.
2. Let go of being caught up in your role or title.
3. Practice the habit of seeking first to understand then to be understood.
4. Embrace the *team* philosophy; Together WE Achieve More
5. Remember the neurochemical benefits of supporting others.
6. Plan for the future, but live the present.
7. Let go of being results-oriented and enjoy the journey of mastering your craft.

Developing an Agile Mindset

In developing high-performing teams, Douglas Smith and John Katzenbach, in their book *The Wisdom of Teams*, recommend that agile teams remain fewer than 12 people per team. This will allow team members to have a more direct conversation and build closer relationships with each other.

Another principle for creating high-performing teams is to create teams where you have groups of generalized specialists. In other words, two or three people within each team can perform each other's tasks. This way, no one role will become a bottleneck for the team. When high-performing teams work in this manner, they tend to be self-directed and self-organizing, set realistic goals, have a shared vision, and create a sense of team identity within their group.

Finally, if you are assuming the role of an agile leader or scrum master and you are also sharing the leadership responsibility with other team members, then you should also practice adaptive leadership. Adaptive leadership is based on the model of situational leadership developed by Ken Blanchard and Paul Percy. They identified four styles of leaders, which are directing, coaching, supporting, and delegating. To learn more about these styles, check out their book *Situational Leadership*.

Assessment Questions

1. What have you learned in this chapter that can help you and your team support each other better?

   _____

   _____

   _____

2. How will you and your team go about using the insight about being surrendered to support that you have learned in this chapter?

   _____

   _____

   _____

3. What steps will you take to implement a more positive surrender to support environment on your current and future projects?

   _____

   _____

   _____

4. What do Sherwin's and David's stories have in common that helped them to be surrendered to support as they pursued their dreams and goals?

   _____

   _____

   _____

5. How can you use the surrendered to support skills we discussed to increase the positive emotions on your team?

   _____

   _____

   _____

Additional Resources

- 5 Ways to Help Your Team Be Open to Change: https://hbr.org/2019/04/5-ways-to-help-your-team-be-open-to-change
- HANDLING SUPPORT ON AGILE TEAMS: https://leadingagile.com/2009/02/handling-support-on-agile-teams/
- The Best Leaders Aren't Afraid to Ask for Help: https://hbr.org/2019/01/the-best-leaders-arent-afraid-to-ask-for-help

CHAPTER 10

Excellence in Execution

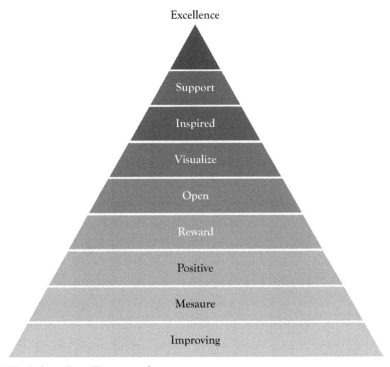

Excellence

Support

Inspired

Visualize

Open

Reward

Positive

Mesaure

Improving

Workplace Jazz Framework

No excuses. No explanation. You don't win on emotion. You win on execution.

—Tony Dungy

Most leaders would agree that they'd be better off having an average strategy with superb execution than a superb strategy with poor execution.

—Stephen Covey

This chapter will introduce you the key factors that enable effective execution of an organization's priorities and how embracing the principle of continuous improvement enables the standard of excellence to be achieved.

According to the *HBR* article "Why Strategy Execution Unravels—and What to Do About It" by Donald Sull, Rebecca Homkes, and Charles Sull, "More than 80 percent of managers say that their goals are limited in number, specific, and measurable and that they have the funds needed to achieve them. If most companies are doing everything right in terms of alignment, why are they struggling to execute their strategies? To find out, we ask survey respondents how frequently they can count on others to deliver on promises—a reliable measure of whether things in an organization get done (see 'Promise-Based Management: The Essence of Execution,' by Donald N. Sull and Charles Spinosa, HBR, April 2007). Fully 84 percent of managers say they can rely on their boss and their direct reports all or most of the time—a finding that would make Drucker proud but sheds little light on why execution fails. When we ask about commitments across functions and business units, the answer becomes clear. Only 9 percent of managers say they can rely on colleagues in other functions and units all the time, and just half say they can rely on them most of the time. Commitments from these colleagues are typically not much more reliable than promises made by external partners, such as distributors and suppliers."

When striving to develop a culture of execution in your agile team, focus on making progress and not perfection; but always strive for excellence. Establish a center of excellence where the top 10–20 percent of project managers will mentor and coach the rest of the teams. Make every effort to make excellence the standard.

It takes more than a verbal commitment to build a high-performing team that can execute. It requires an emotional commitment to the team vision, values, purpose, history, and relationship.

"I never even thought about whether or not they understand what I'm doing ... the emotional reaction is all that matters as long as there's some feeling of communication, it doesn't need to be understood."—John Coltrane

You could develop a world-class agilest mindset, whether you are an athlete, a business manager, a musician, an agile developer, or a scrum manager.

High-Performing Team Secrets from Hans Zimmer— Excellence Is a Character Trait

Hans Zimmer is notably the greatest and the most well-known composer of our time. He has perfected the art of musical scoring for a film that fits the culture and theme of any movie he has written for. Hans Zimmer is a musical genius and composer from Germany. He has written musical scores for:

- Africa: The Serengeti
- Backdraft
- Black Hawk Down
- Cool Runnings
- Gladiator
- Inception
- Interstellar
- Kung Fu Panda
- Man of Steel
- Pearl Harbor
- Pirates of the Caribbean
- Sherlock Holmes
- The Dark Knight Rises
- The Lion King
- Thelma and Louise
- And many more

He has written over 114 movie scores from indie to blockbusters over the past three decades. Check out the following link to view a listing of all of his movie score trailers listed in alphabetical order: http:// ranker.com/ list/hans-zimmer-movie-soundtracks-and-film-scores/reference.

Hans began developing music with his friends Richard Harvey and Nick Glennie-Smith in a studio called the Snake Ranch. It was in the Snake Ranch that Hans Zimmer experimented. He has a deep passion, vision, strong values, and integrity to see orchestral music live on through his composition and film scores.

Hans started working with Nick early on in his musical journey when Nick was a recording engineer at Riverside Recordings in London. Later Hans worked at the Air Edel Agency with his friend Richard Harvey as composers writing TV advertising music. During this time, Hans and Richard also befriended Stanley Myers, the composer. Lebo M. stated that working with Hans created a spirit of brotherhood and a spirit of an unwritten formula happened, which was inspired by the music and the way they worked together.

Hans Zimmer's friends know him as an intimate, funny, intelligent, and brilliant man. When Hans works on a film score with other composers, they write for 12 hours a day, seven days a week, for about four to five months at a time.

Hans Zimmer's vision is to keep orchestral music alive and expose as many people in the world to the amazing sights and sounds through his cinematic film scores. His passion drives everything he does to make a film come alive. His recent concert tour is an example that shows the camaraderie of musicians he is surrounded with that are passionate about music, and that provides the audience with an upfront experience of the power of music.

Hans likes to include other musicians in the decision process when he is determining his vision for a film score, and he seeks their opinion when selecting music for his film score for his live performances. They share ideas and experiment with what works and what does not work. He listens to their input and respects their opinions.

"It makes a big difference if you can fall in love with a project," Hans said.

Hans Zimmer has a set of core values that he uses when composing a movie score. His values are used to determine whom he hires, how he records, what instruments he uses, and how he approaches each movie score. The values are:

- Be clear about your purpose.
- Love what you do.
- Be willing to experiment.
- Work with people that you trust and are experts in their craft.
- Put in the time and work hard.
- Be willing to try something different.
- Face your fears.
- Push the limits of what is possible.
- Work with a coach or a mentor who has been there before.

When you review his list of values, can't you hear it in his film scoring? Think about the movie *Inception*. You can hear him pushing the limits of what is possible, facing his fears to try something new and exciting, and being willing to experiment with new sounds and musical formats.

Hans Zimmer understands what it takes to create buy-in and engagement. When he selects musicians who are recommended by other composers, whom he has worked with, or are recommendations from friends who are experts on their instruments, Hans lets them know what he is looking for from their part and then allows them to use their own genius to fill in their part. Hans met a few of the musicians at a dinner party where they hung out and played music, relaxed, and got to know each other as friends.

- Aleksey Igudesman and Tristan had a string trio call Trilogy.
- Yolanda Charles on electric bass.
- Mary Scully on acoustic bass.
- Satnam Ramgotra, percussionist (Hans allowed Satnam to pick a select group percussionist that he has worked with on other records).
- Guthrie Govan, the guitarist, was discovered on YouTube.
- Johnny Marc, guitarist.
- Czarina Russell, singer and composer.

- Frank Ricotti, marimbas.
- Gary Kettel, timpani.
- Mark Brickman, lighting designer.

Developing a musical score and a great performance require a little exploration. Even though Hans' musical score has all the parts written out with specific direction on what Hans Zimmer wanted to hear, he allowed the talent and experience of his musicians to expand his composition.

All the musicians who have worked with Hans Zimmer work to develop a real relationship with him. He knows their family, their ambitions, their dreams, and their fears. He is more than their boss or employer; he is someone who wants them to succeed and feel valued. So, they, in return, bring their whole selves to every rehearsal, performance, or musical score. The musicians are family, and they all love him for it.

Hans: "I don't want to tell you what to do, you know my music really well, you just do what you want to do. Business at the Speed of Trust."

Hans Zimmer is an amazing composer and interpreter of stories. He is also flexible with his musicians and includes them in the storytelling process. During the development of the *Lion King* score, Richard Harvey was hired to add the flute and wind instrument parts to the score, but was unable to fly over to LA from London during the score development process. Richard and Hans developed the entire score in their studios and exchanged scores and music via DHL shipments. This was before the time you could share large files through e-mail or File Transfer Protocol (FTP) Internet protocols sites.

In developing the film score for *The Dark Knight*, Hans focused his musical motifs on the sounds of the *Joker* and created a sound that viewers would hate, but would also remind them of the Joker character. Hans pushed his musical vocabulary to the edge to create a sound that moviegoers had never heard before using instruments he had developed just for this score. He was able to get inside the mind of the writer and understand the underlining story that made his film score and interpretation of the story into a musical masterpiece.

Today, people want an experience; they want to be surprised, to experience something that they have not considered before. A key to Hans

Zimmer's genius is to keep his musical composition and performance visually interesting by manipulating the film through the use of time. Time can be manipulated by composing music that uses large sound or long notes held by the musicians. Think of the movie *Inception*. The music in *Inception* manipulates the prospection of time in the audience's mind. Hans accomplishes this in *Inception* by leaving the longest notes at the deepest level of the dream state and by increasing the frequency of the notes at the higher level of the dream state. He also allows his musicians to be as creative as they can be within the guiding principles of the culture of the music he is composing for a film.

When rehearsing for the Hans Zimmer concert series, he worked with the section of the band, orchestra, and chorus at a different time to get everyone to learn their part and to work out their interpretation of the part in harmony with the big picture of the piece they were working on and the theme of the entire concert.

During rehearsals, Hans has the group review the score and their parts while listening to the original score recording using music software. This enables the musicians to study their parts while hearing how their parts fit within the larger musical score and perform with a better understanding of the composer's intent for the score.

Hans's rehearsing process was to work with small ensembles of musicians and slowly build up the sound and musical experience he was looking to create. It was an incremental and iterative process that built on a foundation of musical genius. Even though Hans and his musicians were faithful to the music, they interpreted it in a new way to bring a fresh take to performing his musical scores.

Working with other musicians who are experts and geniuses and who are your friends helps each musician raise their game and want to perform and work at a higher level. Everyone is vibing with each other and pushing each other to another level.

Hans has a team of copyists and orchestrators who support his efforts; they have worked with Hans for years. It is interesting to note how loyal Hans Zimmer is to his support staff.

Hans has a special device that makes sounds that we have never heard before. It creates an emotional connection that fits the mood of the scene in the movie, that is, *Man of Steel*.

Most of his movies are scored in a collocated fashion. He works closely with the editors and the cutting room team to edit and fit the music in the right sections of the movie. It is like working on an agile project in a scrum room.

As the leader, Hans Zimmer challenges his musicians to try new things with their instruments. He challenges them to play in new ways and experiment. His focus is to keep the excitement going and keep everyone from feeling bored with their role and their performance. This is a critical essence of his genius. He was pushing his musicians to new levels of performance.

Hans: "People always mistake the idea that a composer is a performer. I am NOT a Performer. You know, I still get stage fright."

You have to invite failure if you are going to succeed and produce something that no one else has composed.

Developing a musical score is like managing an agile project where you have a daily scrum meeting and getting constant feedback from the product owner or film director.

Composing or preparing for a musical concert with Hans is a process that is consistently changing, and the musicians and staff have to be agile and very flexible. They understand that change is a part of the creative process that they must embrace.

In the bestselling book *Managing Transition*, William Bridges, PhD, says, "Your experience as a leader or a manager can be compared to that of someone conducting an orchestra: you have to keep track of the many different instruments, each playing different sequences of notes and each starting or stopping on its own terms. While you keep a sense of the whole piece, you have to shift your attention from one section to another. You need to hold in your mind the overall design of the melody and har-monies, for unless you do that, every little change will sound like a new and unrelated melody that just happened to come along, without any relation to the rest of the music."

To handle continuous change, you need an overall plan or score where the various parts are orchestrated to work together. Realize that continu-ous change is normal, and that growth requires change.

All musicians get better by seeking out and working with others who are much better than they are. This is the essence of growth and fulfillment as a musician. The goal of all great musicians is not perfection but excellence, and excellence can only be obtained from continuous growth from being around others who are better than you.

The Neuroscience of Excellence

Researchers have discovered the secret to peak performance and mind-brain performance. It is a whole-brain integration. Whole-brain integration can be found in peak performance in athletics, business, and music.

Harald S. Hurung found, "The key to peak performance, we have found in our research, is *integrated brain functioning*, as measured by EEG. What this means is that the top-performing brain is more coherent. The various parts of the brain, each of which has different responsibilities, are collaborating in a better way—like the musicians of an orchestra working in concert. The brain is more relaxed and wakeful and more efficient (using less energy to perform a task)." Harald S. Hurung has combined these three different measures into his Brain Integration Scale.

According to the book *World-Class Brain* by Harald S. Hurung, his research also discovered that it "was a surprise to us that the amateur musicians had levels of brain integration that were very similar to the professional musicians: 2.48 for the professionals compared to 2.45 for the amateurs. This was on the same level as that of the world-class athletes (2.5) and top managers (2.48) and significantly higher than for the control athletes and managers—1.3 and 1.54, respectively. At first, we weren't sure what to think. Still, then we realized that it's quite possible that a lifelong pursuit of musical performance is simply good for the brain and develops brain integration irrespective of whether one is amateur or professional."

Side note, one of the grave dangers that we as a society continue to do is when community budgets are tight, the first thing that we do is cut the arts and music out of schools. As you can see, based on research, music provides the development for whole-brain integration, whether someone decides to become a professional musician or performer and plays music for their enjoyment. Music is a part of the liberal arts and provides a full education as well as shapes the brains of leaders of the future.

To develop the ability to become a world-class agile practitioner will require the same focus and mindset needed to be a world-class athlete, musician, or business manager: study, practice, persistence, hard work, and visualization or meditation. It will require developing a fully integrated brain that is comfortable living in the zone. Here are steps you can take to become a world-class agilest.

Developing a World-Class Agilest Mindset

Becoming a world-class performer or developing a world-class organization requires the same mindset that we have learned about from reading Hans Zimmer's story. It requires study, practice, collaborating with other experts, and committing to be a lifelong learner within your craft. You could develop a world-class agilest mindset, whether you are an athlete, a business manager, a musician, an agile developer, or a scrum manager. Following are just a few items that I believe will provide the greatest results for the time spent in these activities. They are:

1. Commit to becoming a lifelong learner in your craft. When one commits to being a lifelong learner, school is never out. You are constantly on the lookout, and hunting for new ideas is the edge that is going to help you get better. The goal is not to compete as if you were in a one-on-one contest with an adversary, but to compete with yourself to be better than you were yesterday. It requires reading books regularly, taking physical as well as online training courses, attending workshops, networking, and collaborating with other experts in your field to talk shop and mull over ideas. Through this process of continuous learning, you will gain new insights and a competitive edge that will allow you to stand out in the market for whatever craft you are striving to be your best at.

2. Deliver value early. Focus on quick wins: Develop a reputation for delivering value early in all of your endeavors. When you develop a reputation for being someone who can deliver value to an organization and your department, you will be someone who is sought out for essential and critical tasks. The agile methodology is based on the premise of delivering value as early in the process as possible and then to continue enhancing the value that you are delivering. The

most excellent jazz musicians in the world are many times not the greatest technicians on their instruments. What makes them great is they have learned to play their role and deliver value to their team in the band much faster than anyone who came before them.

3. Eliminate waste. Waste can be thought of from the standpoint of agile development as uncompleted work, red tape processes, documentation that does not add value, extra features in a product that do not add the core value, and defects that are bugs in a product or service. By being a lifelong learner and delivering value quickly to your customers and clients and learning from other experts, you will pick up on the minute details of what to do. Still, most importantly, you will pick up on the details of what not to do as you deliver value as a world-class agilest.

So, the real question is: Are you willing to pay the price to be world-class?

Are you willing to put in the work, to study, to learn, to reach out to other experts, to spend time visualizing and meditating, and mentally rehearsing your skills and craft? These activities are not for the faint of heart because you can only coast downhill. Rising to the apex of your craft will require hard work, discipline, persistence, and a commitment never to give up. So again, I ask, are you willing to pay the price to build a high-performing agile team?

Assessment Questions

1. What have you learned in this chapter that can help you and your team execute excellently with one another?

   _____

   _____

   _____

2. How will you and your team go about using the insight about executing excellently that you have learned in this chapter?

   _____

   _____

   _____

3. What steps will you take to implement an excellence in execution strategy on your current and future projects?

_____

_____

_____

4. What can you learn from Hans Zimmer's story that can help you pursue your dreams and goals through life's ups and downs?

_____

_____

_____

5. How can you use the agile mindset we discussed to increase your excellence in execution on your team?

_____

_____

_____

Your Workplace Jazz Action Plan

Read: *World-Class Brain* by Harald S. Harung

Additional Resources

- Why Strategy Execution Unravels and What To Do About It: https://hbr.org/2015/03/why-strategy-execution-unravel-sand-what-to-do-about-it
- Unleashing long-term value through operations excellence: https://mckinsey.com/business-functions/operations/our-insights/unleashing-long-term-value-through-operations-excellence
- Smart Leaders Focus on Execution First and Strategy Second: https://hbr.org/2017/11/smart-leaders-focus-on-execution-first-and-strategy-second

CHAPTER 11

How Emotionally Connected Teams Build Trust Through Coaching

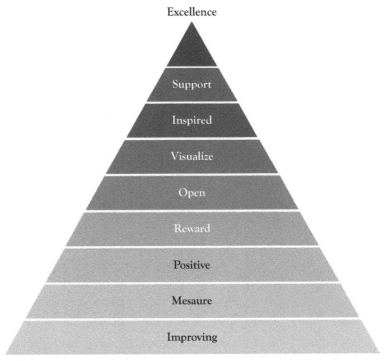

Workplace Jazz Framework

Everyone needs a coach, whether it's a top-level executive, a graduate student, a homemaker, a homeless person, or the President of the United States.

—Anthony Robbins

A coach is someone who tells you what you don't want to hear, who has to see what you don't want to see, so you can be who you always knew you could be.

—Tom Landry

This chapter will illustrate the importance of coaching and its impact on your performance. All great musicians seek coaching from highly accomplished mentors.

Many of the top-performing artists in the world still work with a coach.

Grover Washington Jr. Lived the Culture He Wanted Others to Follow

Donald Robinson, a Grammy-nominated producer and musician, experienced what a leader needs to do to build a culture of excellence in his organization as he shared with me his story of working with the legendary Grover Washington Jr.

Robinson:

I wanted to talk about Grover Washington Jr. and just what a blessing it's been to me.

Wow. I was his music director for 10-plus years. I met him in Philadelphia. I had a publishing deal with EMI at the time, and they recommended that we meet. And he was looking for songs, so I wrote two songs for him, and he ended up picking them for his record. And we just had a great relationship. Great guy. Of course, I knew some of the band members that played with him anyway from Philly.

One of the band members was leaving, and that's when I got a call from him to join his band if I was available. Of course, I jumped at that opportunity, and it was great. I'm going to just share with you about five things that Grover taught me about leadership. What a great guy he was.

One was his playing. He played with so much joy and passion. This guy ... We would be rehearsing, and he would play like he's on stage every time. He would never pick a moment just to be lax and like, "Oh, it's just a rehearsal. We're just going to play a little bit." But this guy would play just with so much passion and joy, and I'll never forget that. It made me take my instrument more seriously, and every time I play, I will think of him and try to evoke that passion and joy that I heard him play with. Even at sound checks, we would get off the bus, traveling all night, and we'd get on stage for soundcheck, and he would just play and play and play like it was 1,000 people in the audience, and it's just a soundcheck. So that's number one, his passion and joy.

Number two is he always made us feel like a band welcome, and he treated us like family. He wasn't the type of guy where, "Okay, I'm staying at this five-star hotel, and, yeah, put the band in Holiday Inn," or something like that. He always made sure that we were treated like family, and wherever he went, he would treat us the same way, when we went out to eat when we stayed in hotels. It just really unified the band in a way where we saw how he treated us in a way that made us feel like family, and it just made us wanna give more.

Number three, he had a mentor's heart. Whenever we would go into a different city, he would find out, find information about the high school, the art school, and he would always invite them to the soundcheck, and he would have them learn about music through him. And this would be pretty much every city that we went in. He would find some high school students, even to the point where he would have them come to the show that night and maybe a young sax player, he would have them come on stage and play with us. But, man, that was just incredible to see how he mentored young people and how much he loved music and education in music, teaching others. They actually named a school in Philadelphia after him, Grover Washington School of the Arts. So he was just an awesome guy when it came to mentoring people, and the heart that he had to teach younger people was terrific.

Number four, I'll tell you a story about an event that happened. We called it the "burning bus tour," because literally, we were in Colorado, I think Denver at the time, on our way to Aspen, the Aspen Jazz Festival, and coming down the hill like 5:30 in the morning, going up and down all those big mountains in Colorado, and the tire ... Actually, the brakes started smoking as the bus was coming down, the tour bus. And what happened was we were all sleeping in our bunks on the tour bus. We hear the bus pull over. The driver runs in the back. We hear hustling going, and he grabs a fire extinguisher and says the tire was smoking, so he sprayed the tire with the fire extinguisher. And the wheel caught on fire. And then we're scrambling to get off the bus. And we all get off the bus, get our clothes and everything and our suitcases, we get off the bus, and the wheel actually went on fire. The whole bus burned down in a matter of 10 minutes.

We're sitting on the side of the road in the mountains, and it's just turning daylight, and the bus is burning. It's on fire. We're looking. We're like, "This is crazy." The fire department took about 25 minutes to get there. By the time they got there, the bus was pretty much done. So, we all get into vans, and we have to figure out another way to get to Aspen, so they take us to this old folk's home in Colorado, and we're there waiting for other transportation to come to pick us up. They got some vans to finish taking us up to the mountains in Aspen.

Grover decides to pull out his horn. We're in an old folk's home. There are all these people sitting around, and he takes his horn out, and he just starts playing. And then they have an upright piano on the side, and I'm playing, and he's playing, and the older people are getting up, and they're dancing, and they're having fun. And we just turned a bad situation into a really good one. People loved it, and he loved it. Man, it was just crazy. So, it was just, again, seeing his heart about how he loved music, and here he is in a place where he can share his music with older people who probably never would've gotten a chance to check him out. Love what he did, and it was great.

Then we get up to Aspen, finally, after all that long day, getting up early in the morning, the burning bus and old folks home. We get up there, and we're high up in the mountains. You know, Aspen, so the air is thin, so you have to really ... You walk a block; you're tired after that because the air is so thin up there. They have oxygen tanks at the side of the stage, so if you get a little dizzy, you go and put the oxygen on, breathe, get some air, and go out. Well, Grover's playing, again, hard as he plays, just with his passion and joy, and he's playing, I think "Let It Flow" or might have been "Mister Magic" something. He's playing, then he'd run to the side and grab the oxygen tank and put it on his face and breathe, and then he comes back out, plays some more, and he'd go back. It was incredible just to see him still putting the passion and the joy into his playing. I'll never forget that.

There are many, many more stories, but the last one is just his integrity and his being a true family man and a musician. And he was loved by many, not only people in the music industry but people all over. His wife Christine and a guy named Paul Silverthorn at the time were his managers. But his children were there. He always encouraged us whenever the band members brought their family over. He encouraged them—just a great guy.

I mean, I can go on and on and on about Grover, but these things stand out: one, his passion and joy; two, how he treated us, as he always welcomed us and treated us like family; three, his heart, being a mentor; and four, just seeing how no matter what the situation was, he made it a good situation. And what it did for me as far as playing is not focused so much on making mistakes, because I would see him do some things and he would just laugh it off and keep going like, "Yeah, whatever." But it helped me to really enjoy the music and not get caught up into just playing it correctly and stressing myself out. I learned that when I'm on or off stage, and I think, "Oh, I can't believe I missed that part," I've learned to let it go. I learned from Grover to just have joy and passion in my playing, and not get caught up in the mistakes. I've learned to enjoy the moment and those things that matter and encourage me to perform at my best.

Donald Robinson is an established presence in the music industry. He spent 10 years as keyboardist and music director for Grover Washington Jr. and has played keyboards with jazz artists such as Gerald Veasley, Kirk Whalum, Kim Waters, Chuck Loeb, Najee, Stevie Wonder, Will Downing, Rick Braun, Walter Beasley, Eric Marienthal, Andy Snitzer, Eric Darius, and many others.

Grover Washington Jr. was a fantastic bandleader, teacher, developer of talent, and coach. Although Donald Robinson and Gerald Veasley were supporting cast and an integral part of Grover's band, he coached and mentored them into becoming the top name jazz musicians they have become today.

In an article titled "The Statistics of Coaching!" by Francois Coetzee, he discovered: "An internal report of the Personnel Management Association showed that when training is combined with coaching, individuals increase their productivity by an average of 86% compared to 22% with training alone. In a study conducted by Metrix Global, companies received an average return of $7.90 for every $1 invested in executive coaching. A Hay Group study of Fortune 500 companies found that 21 to 40% utilize Executive Coaching. The same study reports that Executive Coaching is used as standard leadership development for elite executives and talented up-and-comers."

Coaching, combined with training and development, is the catalyst to help you build a high-performance agile team that can impact your department and organization's bottom line.

Jazz musicians, by nature and nurture, understand the value of coaching. Many of the top-performing artists in the world still work with a coach. Musicians also tend to coach each other throughout their careers and as they collaborate on various musical projects. This is the case across all genres of music. Stop and reflect on the story of Hans Zimmer, David Dyson, Phil Perry, and others mentioned throughout this book.

Certain music, jazz, in particular, has the ability to make you a better citizen of the world. It helps you expand your world view and gives you more confidence in your cultural achievements. Improvisational jazz teaches you about yourself while the swing in jazz teaches you how to work with others.

—Wynton Marsalis

The Neuroscience of Coaching

In an article from the American Psychological Association, entitled "The Neuroscience of Coaching" by Richard E. Boyatzis and Anthony I. Jack stated, "Beyond one-on-one coaching, this issue may predict when and why peer coaching cannot only be effective but may sometimes be more sustained than working with a professional coach. Peer coaching, whether one-on-one or in small groups, functions like what used to be called support groups, or more frequently now called study teams. A small group of people, peers who may or may not be friends before the formation of the group, get together to help each other. The focus is wide, not just on work but on life in general. The quality of the relationships will reveal itself to be the most important factor in these groups working and sustaining their membership. Most organizations cannot afford to hire a sufficient number of professional coaches for all of their managers, let alone all professionals and other staff. Many organizations do not even offer services to all executive-level managers. Under these constraints, peer coaching might be the only method to bring the benefits of coaching to large numbers of people in an organization. It also might hold the promise of changing organizational norms and culture if sufficient numbers of people engage in them. Peer coaching can be a transformative practice for the coach, providing the individual with valuable insight into how effective relationship-based approaches are and so helping to transform their overall management style to resonant leadership."

What Are the Benefits of Coaching?

- Expert guidance. Expert guidance is required when you are seeking a coach. You want to find someone who has real-world experience as well as strategic and innovative ideas that they have gained from continuous study and working on their craft. Think of going on a safari; who would you rather have, someone who gives you a brochure or someone who has been there and can show you all the risks, issues, and dangers to look out for as well as all the beautiful scenery to observe?
- Insight from the coach's background and experience. World-class athletes and musicians continuously seek coaching from coaches who have a well-rounded background with lots of experience. They find someone who has lots of coaching experience and who have seen and corrected the challenges they are facing.
- Better collaboration and communication. When you are working with an experienced coach, you have someone to collaborate and bounce ideas off of. You have someone

who can help you obtain a different perspective from their experience and knowledge, which gives you a competitive advantage.

- Accelerated change and performance. You also reap the benefit of focusing on the items that will make the most significant impact on the change that you are seeking. You, therefore, accelerate the time it takes to get to where you are trying to go and achieve your goals.
- Cost reduction. All world-class athletes and musicians pay a premium price for coaching. But, when compared to the amount of time they save and investments they would have to make to figure this out for themselves, it reduces the cost to accomplish your goals.
- Increase talent capacity and capabilities. Coaching increases the capacity of the person being coached. It helps them accomplish more and improves their capability to get more done in less time. So, by having a dedicated professional coach or engaging in peer-to-peer coaching as we learned in the previous article, your team will be able to accomplish much more by being coached compared to a team that is not.

The Agile Mindset

- Develop an agile coaching team of senior agile practitioners in your organization. Create a book club and invest in training for your coaches.
- Work with an external agile coach who has expert knowledge and real-world experience. You want a coach who is being coached to be a better coach themselves. Yes, even coaches need coaching.
- Develop a peer-to-peer agile coaching team to reduce the cost of coaching and increase your team's capacity and capabilities.
- Remember, world-class athletes, musicians, and business professionals all have coaches, and high-performing teams need a coach too.

Assessment Questions

1. What have you learned in this chapter that can help you and your team provide better coaching for one another?

_____

_____

_____

2. How will you and your team go about using the insight about coaching you have learned in this chapter?

_____

_____

_____

3. What steps will you take to implement a more positive coaching environment on your current and future projects?

_____

_____

_____

4. What can you learn from Grover Washington Jr.'s story to help you become a better coach in pursuing your dreams and goals through life's ups and downs?

_____

_____

_____

5. How can you use the peer-to-peer coaching skills we discussed to increase the positive emotions on your team?

_____

_____

_____

Additional Resources

- What Can Coaches Do for You? https://hbr.org/2009/01/what-can-coaches-do-for-you
- The Neuroscience of Coaching: https://meeco-institute.org/wp-content/uploads/2018/05/The_Neuroscience_of_Coaching1.pdf
- What is an agile coach? A valuable role for organizational change: https://cio.com/article/3294700/agile-coach-role-defined.html

CHAPTER 12

Getting Started with Workplace Jazz and Next Steps

A good quartet is like a good conversation among friends interacting with each other's ideas.

—Stan Getz

Blues is a condition which doesn't change from generation to generation. Every generation discovers it in its own way.

—John Hammond

Change is always happening. That's one of the wonderful things about jazz music.

—Maynard Ferguson

This chapter will help you build a roadmap and steps required to build a workplace jazz culture in your organization.

High-Performing Agile Team Building Is an Ongoing Process

William G. Dyer, W. Gibb Dyer Jr., and Jeffrey H. Dyer, in their book *Team Building*, say, "Team building should be thought of as an ongoing process, not as a single event. People who want to get away for a couple of days and 'do team-building' but then return to doing business, as usual, have an incorrect notion of the purpose of team building. Team building is a meta competency which great teams develop that allows them to evaluate and change the way the organization functions systematically."

It is not a single event; team-building is a daily, weekly, and monthly activity. What are you doing to cultivate your workplace jazz environment as a core value and a part of your organization's operational model?

Gallup Statistics: Where Are You?

According to the Gallup organization, after surveying over 15 million people in the past 30 years, 38 percent of the union employees are engaged and 45 percent of non-union employees are engaged. They have identified 12 key attributes that are predictors that will improve employee engagement and buy-in. These 12 attributes are:

- I know what is expected of me at work.
- I have the materials and equipment I need to do my work right.
- At work, I have the opportunity do what I do best every day.
- In the last seven days, I have received recognition or praise for doing good work.
- My supervisor, or someone at work, seems to care about me as a person.
- There is someone at work who encourages my development.
- At work, my opinions seem to count.
- The mission or purpose of my company makes me feel my job is important.
- My associates or fellow employees are committed to doing quality work.
- I have a best friend at work.
- In the last six months, someone has talked to me about my progress.
- This last year, I have had opportunities to learn and grow.

http://news.gallup.com/businessjournal/122849/employee-engage-ment-labor-relations.aspx

And, according to the Incentive Federation, the Incentive Research Foundation, Maritz, and World at Work:

- 90 percent of business leaders believe that an engagement strategy could positively impact their business, yet only 25 percent of them have a strategy in place.
- 39 percent of employees feel underappreciated at work, with 77 percent reporting that they would work harder if they felt better recognized.

We have a lot of work to do to continue to increase employee engagement and build a workplace jazz environment. Remember, workplace jazz is developing the jazz mindset, an agile mindset, and bringing it into your work culture and creating teams of like-minded agilests where everyone becomes an expert in their craft. At the same time, they understand the bigger vision and the value that they create.

What steps are you taking in your organization to enhance employee engagement?

To achieve great things, two things are needed; a plan and not quite enough time.

—Leonard Bernstein

Next Steps to Creating a High-Performing Agile Project Team Using the IMPROVISE Framework

You Have to Name It to Tame It

In the following table, think of what you or your organization does that is working, not working, or needs improvement under each section.

Next, after you have listed everything you can think of, write the letter F, L, or A next to the items.

F = Fix, L = Leave, and A = Accept

Improving	Reward	Inspired
Measure	Open	Support
Positive	Visualize	Excellence

Once completed, you will have enough information to develop a 3-, 6-, 9-, or 12-month roadmap of activities you and your team can embark on to improve your organization's workplace jazz culture and begin creating your organization's musical score.

Bibliography and Discography

Agile Alliance 2020 "Facilitation." Available Online: https://agilealliance.org/glossary/facilitation/#q=~(infinite~false~filters~(postType~(~'page~'post~'aa_book~'aa_event_session~'aa_experience_report~'aa_glossary~'aa_research_paper~'aa_video)~tags~(~'facilitation))~searchTerm~'~sort~false~sortDirection~'asc~page~1) (accessed on October 19, 2019).

Agile Alliance. 2020. "12 Principles Behind the Agile Manifesto." Available Online: https://agilealliance.org/agile101/12-principles-behind-the-agile-manifesto/ (accessed on October 19, 2019).

Agile Alliance. 2020. "Manifesto for Agile Software Development." Available Online: https://agilealliance.org/agile101/the-agile-manifesto/ (accessed on October 19, 2019).

Agile Skills Project Wiki. 2020. Available Online: https://sites.google.com/site/agileskillsprojectwiki/agile-skills-inventory (accessed on October 19, 2019).

Barrett, K., R. Ashley, D. Strait, N. Kraus. 2013 "US National Library of Medicine National Institutes of Health—Art and science: how musical training shapes the brain." Available Online: https://ncbi.nlm.nih.gov/pmc/articles/PMC3797461/ (accessed on October 19, 2019).

Boyatzis, R., and A. Jack. 2018. "The Neuroscience of Coaching." Available Online: https://meeco-institute.org/wp-content/uploads/2018/05/The_Neuroscience_of_Coaching1.pdf (accessed on October 19, 2019).

Brassey, J., N. Van Dam, and K. Coates. 2019. "Seven Essential Elements of a Lifelong-Learning Mind-Set." Available Online: https://mckinsey.com/business-functions/organization/our-insights/seven-essential-elements-of-a-lifelong-learning-mind-set (accessed on October 19, 2019).

Bridges, PhD, W. 2017. *Managing Transition*. Pennsylvania: Da Capo Press Books.

Brown, B. 2016. "What is Kata?" Available Online: https://continuouscoachingcommitment.com/what-is-kata/ (accessed on October 19, 2019).

Business Dictionary. 2020. Available Online: http://businessdictionary.com/definition/active-listening.html (accessed on October 19, 2019).

Callard, A., 2019. *Aspiration: The Agency of Becoming*. Oxford: Oxford University Press. Kindle Edition.

Coetzee, F. 2018. "The Statistics of Coaching!" Available Online: https://nlpwithpurpose.com/blog/coaching-statistics/ (accessed on October 19, 2019).

DC Bassist David Dyson Interview w/Pieces of a Dream. Available Online: (https://youtu.be/VPcc_or7zMs)." (accessed on October 19, 2019).

Dictionary.com, 2020. "Muse." Available Online: https://dictionary.com/browse/muse (accessed on October 19, 2019).

Doerr, J. 2018. *Measure What Matters.* New York, NY: Penguin Group (USA) LLC.

Doerr, J. 2018. *Measure What Matters: How Google, Bono, and the Gates Foundation Rock the World with OKRs*, 14. New York, NY: Penguin Publishing Group. Kindle Edition.

Dyer, W., G. Dyer, and Jr., J. Dyer. 2013. *Team Building: Proven Strategies for Improving Team Performance*, 5th ed. New York, NY: Wiley & Sons.

Dyson, D., 2020. "David Dyson." Available Online: http://daviddysonbass.com/ (accessed on October 19, 2019).

Elliot, S. 2020. "Getting Started with OKRs For Small Businesses." Available Online: https://gtmhub.com/blog/getting-started-with-okrs-for-small-businesses/ (accessed on October 19, 2019).

Ericsson PhD, K. 2008. "Deliberate Practice and Acquisition of Expert Performance: A General Overview." Available Online: https://online library.wiley.com/doi/full/10.1111/j.1553-2712.2008.00227.x (accessed on October 19, 2019).

Ravel, F. 2020. Available Online: https://lifeintune.com/ (accessed on October 19, 2019).

Gallup-Healthways Well-Being Index. 2020. Available Online: https://gallup.com/cliftonstrengths/en/252137/home.aspx?utm_source=bing&utm_medium=cpc&utm_campaign=new_strengths_ecommerce_brand_search_us&utm_keyword=gallup%20test&utm_source=bing&utm_medium=cpc&utm_campaign=New_Strengths_ECommerce_Brand_Search_US&utm_content=gallup%20test&msclkid=80263926b23215030bbe66239f50bac5 (accessed on October 19, 2019).

GetApp. 2020. "Top 360 Degree Feedback Software." Available Online: https://getapp.com/p/sem/360-degree-feedback-software?t=Top%20360%20Degree%20Feedback%20Software&camp=adw_search&utm_content=g&utm_source=ps-google&utm_campaign=COM_US_Desktop_BE-360_Degree_Feedback&utm_medium=cpc&account_campaign_id=1596693252&account_adgroup_id=89458525193&ad_id=409719498889&gclid=CjwKCAjwmKLzBRBeEiwACCVihpVQzdLwyQlVJTbFNsyrgRz-n4A4BtONsjc3DkAGUUiWTGat67-8WxoCxbIQAvD_BwE (accessed on October 19, 2019).

Glaser, J. 2016. Conversational Intelligence. New York, NY: Taylor and Francis. Kindle Edition.

Glaser, J. 2016. *Conversational Intelligence*, p. 112. New York: Taylor and Francis. Kindle Edition.

Griffiths, M., 2015 *PMI-ACP Exam Prep*. United States of America: RMC Publication, pp.178–84.

Handscomb, C., A. Jaenicke, K. Kaur, B. McCall, and A. Zaidi. 2018. "How to Mess Up Your Agile Transformation in Seven Easy (Mis)Steps." Available Online: https://mckinsey.com/business-functions/organization/our-insights/how-to-mess-up-your-agile-transformation-in-seven-easy-missteps (accessed on October 19, 2019).

Hurung, H. 2018. "World-Class Brain." Iowa: Brian Integration Systems.

Hyken, S. 2020. "Shep Hyken." Available Online: https://hyken.com/who-is-shep/ (accessed on October 19, 2019).

Jean Tabaka, J. 2006. *Collaboration Explained: Facilitation Skills for Software Project Leaders*. New Jersey: Addison-Wesley Professional; 1 Edition.

Kosfeldl, M., 2007. "Trust in the Brain Neurobiological Determinants of Human Social Behavior." Available Online: https://ncbi.nlm.nih.gov/pmc/articles/PMC3327534/ (accessed on October 19, 2019).

Lieberman, M. 2013 "Social: Why Our Brains Are Wired to Connect." Dr. Matthew D. Lieberman Social (pp. 77–78). USA, Crown. Kindle Edition.

Loeb, C. 2020 "Chuck Loeb." Available Online: https://en.wikipedia.org/wiki/Chuck_Loeb (accessed on October 19, 2019).

MacKay, J. 2018. "Deliberate Practice: What it is and how to use it to Find Flow and Improve Any Skill." Available Online: https://blog.rescuetime.com/deliberate-practice/ (accessed on October 19, 2019).

Mergner, L. 2019. "Chuck Loeb, Guitarist and Composer, Dies at 61." Available Online: https://jazztimes.com/features/tributes-and-obituaries/chuck-loeb-guitarist-composer-dies-61/ (accessed on October 19, 2019).

Merriam Webster. 2020. "Surrender." Available Online: https://merriam-webster.com/dictionary/surrender (accessed on October 19, 2019).

Merriam Webster. 2020. Available Online: https://merriam-webster.com/dictionary/aspiration (accessed on October 19, 2019).

Onderick-Harvey, E., 2019. "5 Ways to Help Your Team Be Open to Change." Available Online: https://hbr.org/2019/04/5-ways-to-help-your-team-be-open-to-change (accessed on October 19, 2019).

Perry, P. 2020. "Phil Perry Music." Available Online: https://philperrymusic.com/ (accessed on October 19, 2019).

Phillips, D. 1993. *Lincoln On Leadership*. New York, NY: Warner Books.

Pillay, S. 2014. 3 "Reasons You Underestimate Risk." Available Online: https://hbr.org/2014/07/3-reasons-you-underestimate-risk (accessed on October 19, 2019).

Rayburn, M. 2020. "To Learn more about Mike Rayburn." Available Online: https://mikerayburn.com/about/ (accessed on October 19, 2019).

Ritvo M.D.E. 2014. Psychology Today "The Neuroscience of Giving: Proof that helping others helps you." Available Online: https://psychologytoday.com/us/blog/vitality/201404/the-neuroscience-giving (accessed on October 19, 2019).

Robinson, D. 2020. "To learn more about Donald Robinson." Available Online: https://sowmusiconline.org/donald-robinson (accessed on October 19, 2019).

Rosenthal, T. 1996. "How Jazz Pianists Practice." Available Online: http://tedrosenthal.com/practice.htm (accessed on October 19, 2019).

Sull, D., R. Homkes, and C., Sull. 2015. "Why Strategy Execution Unravels—and What to Do About It." Available Online: https://hbr.org/2015/03/why-strategy-execution-unravelsand-what-to-do-about-it (accessed on October 19, 2019).

Turkel, B. 2020. "Bruce Turkel." Available Online: https://bruceturkel.com (accessed on October 19, 2019).

Tyler, J., 2009. "Employee Engagement and Labor Relations." Available Online: http://news.gallup.com/businessjournal/122849/employee-engagement-labor-relations.aspx (accessed on October 19, 2019).

Veasley, G. 2020. "To learn more about Gerald Veasley." Available Online: https://geraldveasley.com/ (accessed on October 19, 2019).

Watchworthy, R. 2019. "List of Films Scored By Hans Zimmer." Available Online: (http://ranker.com/list/hans-zimmer-movie-soundtracks-and-film-scores/reference) (accessed on October 19, 2019).

Wellington, A., 2020. "Anthony Wellington Teaches Rhythm using The Rhythm Yardstick." Available Online: https://youtu.be/8Sw_trDFJw8 (accessed on July 23, 2020).

Wellington, A. 2020. "Anthony Wellington." Available Online: http://bassology.net/ (accessed on July 23, 2020).

West, S. 2013. "Freddie Ravel Interview by Shannon West for Smooth Views Magazine." Available Online: http://smoothviews.com/interviews/ravel1209.htm (accessed on October 19, 2019).

Westfall, J., and J. Jasper. 2012. "Inaction Inertia, the Sunk Cost Effect, and Handedness: Avoiding the Losses of Past Decisions." Available Online: https://ncbi.nlm.nih.gov/pubmed/22898591 (accessed on October 19, 2019).

Whalum,K., 2020. "Kirk Whalum." Available Online: https://kirkwhalum.com/ (accessed on October 19, 2019).

White, S. 2018. "4 Interesting Myths and Facts about the Mozart Effect." Available Online: https://dinnertablemba.com/the-mozart-effect/ (accessed on October 19, 2019).

Wooten, V. 2020. "Victor Wooten." Available Online: https://victorwooten.com/ (accessed on July 23, 2020).

Zenger, J., and J. Folkman. 2013. "Overcoming Feedback Phobia: Take the First Step." Available Online: https://hbr.org/2013/12/overcoming-feedback-phobia-take-the-first-step (accessed on October 19, 2019).

Zimmerman, E. 2016. "Survey Shows Visualizing Success Works." by Available Online: https://forbes.com/sites/eilenezimmerman/2016/01/27/survey-shows-visualizing-success-works/#1fba64f4760b (accessed on October 19, 2019).

About the Author

Gerald J. Leonard is currently the President and CEO of Principles of Execution (PofE), a Strategic Project Portfolio Management and IT Governance consulting practice based in the Metro Washington, DC, area. He attended Central State University in Ohio, where he received his bachelor's in music degree and later earned a master's in music for classical bass from the Cincinnati Conservatory of Music. After graduation, Gerald moved to New York City, where he worked as a professional bassist and studied with the late David Walters, distinguished professor of double bass at both the Juilliard and Manhattan schools of music.

While living in Manhattan, Gerald worked as a full-time minister for the New York City Church of Christ and managed time to fulfill numerous music engagements. After resigning from his ministry position, he was able to devote more time to his music career and spend more quality time with his family.

Several years later, Gerald began his information technology (IT) career, focusing initially on network computing and project management. During the last 20+ years, he has worked as an IT Project Management consultant and earned his PfMP, PMP, MCSE, MCTS, CQIA, COBIT Foundation, Certified Conversational Intelligence (C-IQ) Coach, and ITIL Foundation certifications. He has acquired certifications in Project Management and Business Intelligence from the University of California, Berkeley; Theory of Constraints Portfolio Management Technical Expert from the Goldratt Institute, Hoshin Kanri Strategic Planning; Executive Leadership Certification from Cornell University; and The Wharton School: Entrepreneurship Acceleration Program.

In his leisure time, Gerald loves playing golf, traveling internationally, and playing his upright bass on special occasions.

To learn more about Gerald, visit www.geraldjleonard.com

Index

OTHER TITLES IN THE PORTFOLIO AND PROJECT MANAGEMENT COLLECTION

Timothy J. Kloppenborg, Xavier University, Editor

- *Stakeholder-led Project Management, Second Edition* by Louise M. Worsley
- *Hybrid Project Management* by Mark Tolbert, and Susan Parente
- *A.G.I.L.E. Thinking Demystified* by Frank Forte
- *Design: A Business Case* by Brigitte Borja de Mozota, and Steinar Valade-Amland
- *Discoveries Through Personal Agility* by Raji Sivaraman, and Michal Raczka
- *Project Communications* by Connie Plowman, and Jill Diffendal
- *Quantitative Tools of Project Management* by David L. Olson
- *The People Project Triangle* by Stuart Copeland, and Andy Coaton
- *How to Fail at Change Management* by James Marion and John Lewis
- *Core Concepts of Project Management* by David L. Olson
- *Projects, Programs, and Portfolios in Strategic Organizational Transformation* by James Jiang, Gary Klein, and Wayne Huang
- *Capital Project Management, Volume III* by Robert N. McGrath
- *Capital Project Management, Volume II* by Robert N. McGrath
- *Capital Project Management, Volume I* by Robert N. McGrath
- *Executing Global Projects* by James Marion, and Tracey Richardson

Concise and Applied Business Books

The Collection listed above is one of 30 business subject collections that Business Expert Press has grown to make BEP a premiere publisher of print and digital books. Our concise and applied books are for...

- Professionals and Practitioners
- Faculty who adopt our books for courses
- Librarians who know that BEP's Digital Libraries are a unique way to offer students ebooks to download, not restricted with any digital rights management
- Executive Training Course Leaders
- Business Seminar Organizers

Business Expert Press books are for anyone who needs to dig deeper on business ideas, goals, and solutions to everyday problems. Whether one print book, one ebook, or buying a digital library of 110 ebooks, we remain the affordable and smart way to be business smart. For more information, please visit www.businessexpertpress.com, or contact sales@businessexpertpress.com.